GOD'S
GREATEST
GIFTS

Other books by St. Thomas Aquinas
available from Sophia Institute Press:

Devoutly I Adore Thee
Light of Faith: The Compendium of Theology
The Three Greatest Prayers

St. Thomas Aquinas

GOD'S GREATEST
GIFTS

*Commentaries on the
Commandments and the Sacraments*

Foreword by Ralph McInerny
The Michael P. Grace Professor of Medieval Studies
University of Notre Dame

SOPHIA INSTITUTE PRESS
Manchester, New Hampshire

The Commentaries published here as GOD'S GREATEST GIFTS were originally translated into English by Joseph B. Collins and included in THE
CATECHETICAL INSTRUCTIONS OF ST. THOMAS AQUINAS, published in
1939 by Joseph F. Wagner, Inc., in New York and by B. Herder, Inc., in
London. In 1992, Sophia Institute Press published an edition that was
based on the earlier Collins translation, but with numerous revisions to
elimate awkward, obscure, or archaic language, to correct errors in the
text and in the references, and to include headings and subheadings not
found in the original translation. This 1997 paperback edition is a reprint
of the 1992 edition.

Sophia Institute Press®
Box 5284, Manchester, NH 03108
1-800-888-9344
http:\ \www.sophiainstitute.com

Library of Congress Cataloging-in-Publication Data

Thomas, Aquinas, Saint, 1225?-1274.
    [De decem praeceptis. English]
    God's greatest gifts: commentaries on the commandments and the
sacraments / St. Thomas Aquinas ; foreword by Ralph McInerny.
        p.   cm.
Translation of: De decem praeceptis and De sacramentis ecclesiae.
ISBN 0-918477-12-3 (cloth) — ISBN 0-918477-53-0 (pbk.)
    1. Ten commandments — Early works to 1800. 2. Sermons, English.
3. Catholic Church — Sermons. 4. Sacraments — Catholic Church — Early
works to 1800. I. Thomas, Aquinas, Saint, 1225?-1274. De sacramentis ecclesiae. English. 1992. II. Title.
BV4655.T52313 1992
241.5'2 — dc20   91-42376 CIP

97 98 99 00 01 10 9 8 7 6 5 4 3 2 1

TABLE OF CONTENTS

THE SACRAMENTS

FOREWORD
Ralph McInerny, Ph.D.
The Michael P. Grace Professor of Medieval Studies
University of Notre Dame

Aquinas the teacher

Most of the images we have of St. Thomas Aquinas show him in his role as Master of Theology, explaining Scripture or other authoritative texts to students who are already highly educated. These scholarly tasks were performed in Latin and many manuscripts of St. Thomas's writings have come down to us — sometimes exclusively in his own hand; sometimes in the hand of one of the secretaries assigned to him — in the Latin that was the learned language of the day.

The *Summa theologiae*, the most famous of his works, is a summary of sacred science for beginners and, if Leonard Boyle, O.P., is right, was destined not so much for beginners in the Faculty of Theology as for beginners in the *studia* of his own order. Their chief vocational concern would be pastoral care, preaching, and evangelizing the faithful.

Aquinas the preacher

St. Thomas himself sometimes engaged in such direct pastoral activity, a fact that is clear from many of his sermons (such as those on the Decalogue published here), as well as from his short work on the Sacraments (also published here). These attest in different ways to St. Thomas's understanding of the role of the theologian and of the continuity that must exist between sacred theology and the faith of the simple.

Aquinas on the Commandments

St. Thomas's sermons on the Commandments were very likely delivered in Naples during Lent of 1273, the year before he died. They were given in his native dialect, written down by Peter d'Andria, and have come down to us in a Latin version.

Now just about every element of the preceding paragraph has been disputed by some scholars. Discussion sometimes turns on what is meant by his native tongue in the documents. (We are told St. Thomas was unable to learn other vernacular languages because of his intense concentration on his theological studies, yet could he have been understood in Naples — to say nothing of Rome or Milan — if he had preached the language he had learned at his mother's knee?) It is also not absolutely certain that these sermons were given in Naples, nor is it certain that they were delivered in 1273.

Yet, after advancing arguments against the time, place, and language given here, Rev. J.P. Torrell (editor of the critical Leonine edition of the sermons on the Decalogue), ends by saying that there are no conclusive reasons to adopt another view.

For us, this scholarly discussion does serve to make us aware of one important fact: St. Thomas preached fairly often in his native tongue and in a variety of places.

Often what comes down to us as the work of a medieval master was neither written nor dictated by the author himself, but consists instead of notes taken down by another on what the master said. When such a version of his teaching was reviewed, revised, and authorized by the master, it had far more authority than one that was simply another's account of what was said. The account of these sermons on the Commandments put into Latin by Peter d'Andria was not seen or corrected by St. Thomas. Accordingly, it is called a *reportatio* rather than a *lectura*. Nonetheless, they are a precious record of the Common Doctor of the Church speaking to the simple faithful about the most basic matters of Christian belief in a language that all can understand.

Aquinas on the sacraments

The little treatise on the sacraments (published in this volume) is usually paired with another, that on the articles of faith, both of which were written in response to a request from the Archbishop of Parma. In this, they are like a great many of St. Thomas's lesser works: we are reading his response to a request for a clarification or for a summary that would advance the pastoral work of the Church. There seems little doubt that St. Thomas saw such responses as part of his professional duty as a Master of Theology.

Given its addressee and its purpose, the treatise on the sacraments of the Church is pitched at a somewhat higher level than the sermons on the Commandments. It was originally composed in Latin, and a slight echo of the university dispute can be heard in the inclusion of a discussion of errors alongside discussion of the true doctrine.

We have a number of extended treatments of the sacraments by St. Thomas and — although this little treatise could not replace them — it manages to put the essence of the theology of the sacraments in a few pages. In fact, this treatise is a marvel of clarity and compression. St. Thomas recalls from St. Augustine the notion and definition of *sacrament* and then shows what the sacraments have in common as well as the ways in which they differ (e.g., some are received but once, whereas the rest can be received more than once).

Noteworthy in St. Thomas's explanations, whether sophisticated or simple, is his reliance on Scripture and the most basic human experiences as a point of reference for the spiritual. For example, in these pages he notes that like biological life, the Christian life must engendered, nurtured, and sustained. Bruises must be bandaged; illness requires medicine. Thus he places before us Baptism, Confirmation, and the Eucharist as the means, respectively, for beginning, perfecting, and sustaining the life of grace. Penance and the Anointing of the Sick restore health to the soul. Matrimony ensures that there will be new members of the Church, and Holy Orders that there will be ministers of the sacraments.

St. Thomas shows that as sensible signs of inward grace, the sacraments have as their form a *verbal formula* and as their matter a *sensible reality* — water, bread, oil. In Christ, the Word is present in the flesh; so, too, in the sacraments the verbal formulas are complemented by the sensible matter. The sacraments thus underscore the incarnational character of Christianity. When they are performed by an appropriate minister with the intention of doing what the Church intends by the sacrament, they produce grace.

St. Thomas Aquinas is the poet of the Eucharist. In these pages, he notes that just as Christ's divinity was hidden from his contemporaries, so, too, today His humanity is hidden from us in the consecrated bread and wine. The matter of the Eucharist is unleavened bread; its form, the words of consecration. The first effect of the consecration is that the bread and wine truly become the body and blood of Jesus Christ; the second effect is that the sacrament unites us with Christ.

St. Thomas Aquinas is one of the clearest and most authoritative of theological voices. During his lifetime and ever since, his work has been at the service of the Magisterium. Whether in his sophisticated treatises or in his vernacular sermons, he was engaged in that Dominican task which is as well the task of every believer: to hear the word of God and — chiefly by keeping it — to make it known to others.

EDITOR'S PREFACE

Although today the wisdom of St. Thomas Aquinas is considered the realm of scholars, much of his work was not meant for scholars, but for the average man struggling to deepen his faith and live a holy life. These commentaries on the Commandments, for example, are derived from Lenten sermons St. Thomas preached to the townspeople of Naples in 1273.

In the spirit of St. Thomas who intended his Lenten sermons for the unlettered as well as the lettered, I have prepared this edition specifically to introduce the wisdom of this great saint and theologian to the average modern reader.

Most people — laymen and scholars alike — find that their first obstacle in reading St. Thomas is the richness of his texts. You will discover that even in these sermons for the average man, St. Thomas has included so many points that it is easy to get lost. (For example, this relatively brief book contains over 350 Scriptural references!)

To help you overcome this obstacle and profit from this incredibly rich text, I have made a number of significant changes in the earlier English translation on which this present edition is based.

First, I have adopted a somewhat unique format. Where necessary, I have added headings and subheadings (in bold-faced type) and have sometimes also rendered in bold-faced type the beginnings of paragraphs. Although this latter may seem typographically odd, it serves an important function: bold-faced passages constitute an outline within the text itself and also correspond directly to entries found in the more-detailed outlines in the Appendix. If you follow the outlines as you read the text, you will never lose your place and will see relations between passages that might otherwise not be apparent.

In addition to adopting a unique format, I have taken other steps to increase this text's readability: some of the longer sentences have been shortened; implied referents have often been made specific; extremely awkward formulations have been rephrased; and the archaic language of the 1939 English edition has been changed into standard modern English.

Where possible, I have given more precise references than were found in the earlier edition. Where that edition indicated that passages are quotations but failed to provide a source, I have retained quotation marks but have similarly indicated no source.

The Scripture quotations in this edition are based on the Douay-Rheims translation of the Bible because the text of that translation closely approximates the text that St. Thomas seems to have been working from. The Douay translation sometimes employs archaic names of books of the Bible or does not use currently accepted enumerations. Where this occurs, I have indicated in parentheses the modern names and numbers as found in the Revised Standard Version (RSV) of the Bible according to the *New Oxford Annotated Bible with the Apocrypha* (New York: Oxford University Press, 1977). Also, where passages from the Douay-Rheims translation are obscure in their meaning, I have occasionally replaced them with the same passages from the Revised Standard Version.

As you read these pages, it is important that you keep in mind that *this is not a scholarly edition nor does it pretend to be*. Scholars should read these sermons in Latin! This edition is for the average person who seeks to know more about his Faith and to grow holy.

Read it slowly, attentively, and prayerfully. You will soon discover why St. Thomas Aquinas was proclaimed a Doctor of the Universal Church in 1567 and why he has been revered as a master theologian for seven centuries.

More importantly, you yourself will grow wise in your Faith and, if you persist in living by that wisdom, you will soon come to be like St. Thomas not only in wisdom, but in holiness.

THE COMMANDMENTS

THE
COMMANDMENTS[1]

1.
THOU SHALT NOT HAVE STRANGE GODS BEFORE ME.

2.
THOU SHALT NOT TAKE THE NAME
OF THE LORD THY GOD IN VAIN.

3.
REMEMBER THAT THOU KEEP HOLY THE SABBATH DAY.

4.
HONOR THY FATHER AND THY MOTHER.

5.
THOU SHALT NOT KILL.

6.
THOU SHALT NOT COMMIT ADULTERY.

7.
THOU SHALT NOT STEAL.

8.
THOU SHALT NOT BEAR FALSE WITNESS
AGAINST THY NEIGHBOR.

9.
THOU SHALT NOT COVET THY NEIGHBOR'S GOODS.

10.
THOU SHALT NOT COVET THY NEIGHBOR'S WIFE.

---

[1] Exod. 20:2-17 and Deut. 5:6-21 list all the Commandments. St. Thomas places the Tenth Commandment (in the present traditional enumeration) before the Ninth. The Tenth Commandment is wider in extension than the Ninth, which is specific.

THE FIRST COMMANDMENT

Thou shalt not have strange gods before me.

The First Commandment which relates to the love of God is: *Thou shalt not have strange gods before me.* For an understanding of this Commandment, we must know how it was violated in earlier times.

A. How the First Commandment was violated

1. Some people worshipped demons: "All the gods of the Gentiles are devils."[2] This is the greatest and most detestable of all sins. Even now there are many who transgress this Commandment, such as those who practice divinations and fortune-telling. Such things, according to St. Augustine, cannot be done without some kind of pact with the Devil. "I would not that you should be made partakers with devils."[3]

2. Some worshipped the heavenly bodies, believing the stars to be gods: "They have imagined the sun and the moon to be the gods that rule the world."[4] For this reason Moses forbade the Jews to raise their eyes or adore the sun, moon, and stars: "Keep

---

[2] Ps. 95:5 (Revised Standard Version: Ps. 96:5)
[3] 1 Cor. 10:20
[4] Wisd. of Sol. 13:2

3

therefore your souls carefully . . . lest perhaps lifting up thine eyes to heaven, thou see the sun, the moon, and all the stars of heaven, and being deceived by error, thou adore and serve them which the Lord thy God created for the service of all the nations."[5] The astrologers sin against this Commandment in that they say that these bodies are the rulers of souls, when in truth they were made for the use of man whose sole ruler is God.

3. Some worshipped the lower elements: "They imagined the fire or the wind . . . to be gods."[6] Into this error also fall those who wrongly use the things of this earth and love them too much: ". . . covetous persons (who serve idols). . . ."[7]

4. Some worshipped their ancestors (for three reasons):

a. From their carnal nature
"For a father being afflicted with a bitter grief made to himself the image of his son who was quickly taken away; and him who then had died as a man, he began now to worship as a god, appointing him rites and sacrifices among his servants."[8]

b. Because of flattery
Being unable to worship certain men in their presence, they, bowing down, honored them in their absence by making statues of them and worshipping one for the other: "Whom they had a mind to honor . . . they made an image . . . that they might honor as present him that was absent."[9] Of such

---

[5] Deut. 4:15,19
[6] Wisd. of Sol. 13:2
[7] Eph. 5:5
[8] Wisd. of Sol. 14:15
[9] Wisd. of Sol. 14:17

also are those men who love and honor other men more than God: "He that loveth his father and mother more than me is not worthy of me."[10] "Put your trust not in princes nor in the children of man, in whom there is no salvation."[11]

c. From presumption
Some, because of their presumption, had themselves called gods. Such, for example, was Nebuchadnezzar.[12] "Thy heart is lifted up and thou hast said, 'I am God.' "[13]

d. From desire for pleasure
Such also are those who believe more in their own pleasures than in the precepts of God. They worship themselves as gods, for by seeking the pleasures of the flesh they worship their own bodies instead of God: "Their god is their belly."[14] We must therefore avoid all these things.

B. Reasons why we should adore one God
As we have already said, the First Commandment forbids us to worship other than the one God: *Thou shalt not have strange gods before me*. There are five reasons for this:

1. God's dignity
The first reason is the dignity of God which, were it belittled in any way, would be an injury to God. We see something similar to this in the customs of men. Reverence is due to every degree of dignity. Thus, a traitor to the king is he who robs him of what

[10] Matt. 10:37
[11] Ps. 145:2-3 (RSV: Ps. 146:3)
[12] Jth. 3:13 (RSV: Jth. 3:8)
[13] Ezek. 28:2
[14] Phil. 3:19

he ought to maintain. Such, too, is the conduct of some toward God: "They changed the glory of the incorruptible God into the likeness of the image of a corruptible man."[15]

This is highly displeasing to God: "I will not give my glory to another, nor my praise to graven things."[16] For it must be known that the dignity of God consists in His omniscience, since the name of God (*Deus*) is from "seeing"; and this is one of the signs of divinity: "Show the things that are to come hereafter and we shall know that ye are gods."[17] "All things are naked and open to His eyes."[18] But this dignity of God is denied Him by practitioners of divination, and of them it is said: "Should not the people seek of their God? Should they consult the dead on behalf of the living?"[19]

2. God's bounty

We also should worship only God because we receive every good from Him. This also is of the dignity of God, that He is the maker and giver of all good things: "When Thou openest Thy hand, they shall all be filled with good."[20] And this is implied in the name of God (*Deus*) which is said to be "distributor" (that is, *dator*) of all things, because He fills all things with His goodness. You are indeed ungrateful if you do not appreciate what you have received from Him and, furthermore, if you make for yourself another god as the sons of Israel made an idol after they had been brought out of Egypt: "I will go after my lovers."[21]

[15] Rom. 1:23
[16] Isa. 42:8
[17] Isa. 41:23
[18] Heb. 4:13
[19] Isa. 8:19
[20] Ps. 103:28 (RSV: Ps. 104:28)
[21] Hos. 2:5

We do this also when we put too much trust in someone other than God, such as may occur when we seek help from another: "Blessed is the man whose hope is in the name of the Lord."[22] Thus, the Apostle says: "Now that you have known God . . . how can you turn again to the weak and needy elements? . . . You observe days and months and times and years."[23]

3. The strength of our promise

The third reason we should worship the one God is taken from our solemn promise. For we have renounced the Devil and we have promised fidelity to God alone. This is a promise which we cannot break: "A man making void the Law of Moses dieth without mercy under two or three witnesses. How much more think ye he deserveth punishment who hath trodden under foot the Son of God, hath esteemed unclean the blood of the testament by which he was sanctified, and hath offered an affront to the Spirit of grace!"[24] "Whilst her husband liveth, she shall be called an adulteress, if she be with another man."[25] Woe, then, to the sinner who enters the land by two ways and who "halts between two sides."[26]

4. The terrible burden of serving the Devil

The fourth reason we should worship the one God is because of the great burden that is imposed on us by service to the Devil: "You shall serve strange gods day and night, who will give you no rest."[27] The Devil is not satisfied with leading us to one sin, but tries to lead us on to others: "Whosoever sins shall be a slave

[22] Ps. 39:5 (RSV: Ps. 40:4)
[23] Gal. 4:9,10
[24] Heb. 10:28-29
[25] Rom. 7:3
[26] 3 Kings 18:21 (RSV: 1 Kings 18:21)
[27] Jer. 16:13

of sin."[28] It is, therefore, not easy for us to escape from the habit of sin. Thus St. Gregory says: "The sin which is not remitted by penance soon draws man into another sin."[29] The very opposite of all this is true of service to God, for His Commandments are not a heavy burden: "My yoke is sweet and my burden is light."[30] A person is considered to have done enough if he does for God as much as he has done for the sake of sin: "For as you have yielded your members unto iniquity to serve uncleanness and iniquity, so now yield your members to serve justice unto sanctification."[31] But on the contrary, it is written of those who serve the Devil: "We wearied ourselves in the way of iniquity and destruction and have walked through hard ways."[32] And again: "They have labored to commit iniquity."[33]

5. The greatness of the reward

The fifth reason we should worship the one God is taken from the greatness of the reward or prize. In no law are such rewards promised as in the law of Christ. To the Mohammedans are promised rivers flowing with milk and honey; to the Jews, the Promised Land; but to Christians, the glory of the angels: "They shall be as the angels of God in Heaven."[34] It was with this in mind that St. Peter asked: "Lord, to whom shall we go? Thou hast the words of eternal life."[35]

---

[28] John 8:34
[29] St. Gregory the Great, *Homily 11 on Ezekiel*, 24
[30] Matt. 11:30
[31] Rom. 6:19
[32] Wisd. of Sol. 5:7
[33] Jer. 9:5
[34] Matt. 22:30
[35] John 6:68

II

THE SECOND COMMANDMENT
Thou shalt not take the name of the Lord thy God in vain.

This is the Second Commandment of the Law. Just as there is but one God we must worship, so there is but one God we should revere in a special manner. This, first of all, has reference to the name of God: *Thou shalt not take the name of the Lord thy God in vain.*

A. The meanings of *in vain*

1. *Vain* can mean "false"
"They have spoken vain things every one to his neighbor."[36] Therefore, we take the name of God in vain when we use it to confirm that which is not true: "Love not a false oath."[37] "Thou shalt not live because thou hast spoken a lie in the name of the Lord."[38] Any one so doing injures God, himself, and all men.

a. Falsehood insults God
It is an insult to God because, when you swear by God, you call Him to witness; and when you swear falsely, you either believe God to be ignorant of the truth (and thus you ascribe

---

[36] Ps. 11:3 (RSV: Ps. 12:2)
[37] Zech. 8:17
[38] Zech. 13:3

ignorance to God, whereas "all things are naked and open to His eyes"[39]) or you think that God loves a lie, whereas He hates it: "Thou wilt destroy all that speak a lie."[40] Or, again, you detract from His power, as if He were not able to punish a lie.

b. Falsehood injures the teller

Likewise, he who swears falsely injures himself, for he binds himself to the judgment of God. To say, "By God, this is so," is the same as to say, "May God punish me if it is not so!"

c. Falsehood injures others

Finally, he who swears falsely injures other men. For there can be no lasting society unless men believe one another. Matters that are doubtful may be confirmed by oaths: "An oath in confirmation puts an end to all controversy."[41]

Therefore, he who violates this precept injures God, is cruel to himself, and harms other men.

2. *Vain* can mean "useless"

"The Lord knoweth the thoughts of men, that they are vain."[42] Therefore, God's name is taken in vain when it is used to confirm things needlessly.

In the Old Law it was forbidden to swear falsely: "Thou shalt not take the name of the Lord thy God in vain."[43] And Christ forbade the taking of oaths except in case of necessity: "You have

---

[39] Heb. 4:13
[40] Ps. 5:7 (RSV: Ps. 5:6)
[41] Heb. 6:16
[42] Ps. 93:11
[43] Deut. 5:11

heard that it was said to them of old, 'Thou shalt not forswear thyself. . . .' But I say to you, do not swear at all."[44] And the reason is that in no part of our body are we so weak as in the tongue, for "the tongue no man can tame."[45] Thus, even in light matters we can perjure ourselves. "Let your speech be: Yea, yea; no, no. . . . But I say to you, do not swear at all."[46]

Note well that an oath is like medicine, which is never taken continually but only in times of necessity. Hence the Lord adds: "And that which is over and above these is evil."[47] "Let not the mouth be accustomed to swearing, for in it there are many falls. And let not the name of God be usual in thy mouth, and meddle not with the names of saints. For thou shalt not escape free from them."[48]

3. *Vain* can signify "sin" or "injustice"

"O ye sons of men, how long will you be dull of heart? Why do you love vanity?"[49] Therefore, he who swears that he will commit a sin takes the name of his God in vain. Justice consists in doing good and avoiding evil. Therefore, if you take an oath that you will steal or commit some crime of this sort, you sin against justice. And although you must not keep this oath, you are still guilty of perjury. Herod did this against John.[50] It is likewise against justice when a person swears *not* to do some good act, as not to enter a church or a religious community. And although this oath, too, is not binding, yet, despite this, the person himself is a perjurer.

[44] Matt. 5:33-34
[45] James 3:8
[46] Matt. 5:37,34
[47] Matt. 5:37
[48] Ecclus. 23:9-10 (RSV: Sir. 23:9-10)
[49] Ps. 4:3 (RSV: Ps. 4.2)
[50] Mark 6

B. Taking God's name in vain

1. False oaths

A person cannot, therefore, swear to a falsehood, swear without good reason, or in any way swear against justice: "And thou shalt swear, 'As the Lord liveth,' in truth, in judgment, and in justice."[51]

2. Foolish oaths

Sometimes *vain* also means foolish: "All men are vain in whom there is not the knowledge of God."[52] Accordingly, he who by blasphemy takes the name of God foolishly, takes the name of God in vain: "And he that blasphemeth the name of the Lord, dying let him die."[53]

C. Taking God's name justly

Thou shalt not take the name of the Lord thy God in vain. However, the name of God may be taken justly for six purposes.

1. To confirm something that is said (as in an oath), we may take God's name justly. In this we show that God alone is the first truth and we also show due reverence to God. For this reason it was commanded in the Old Law that one must not swear except by God.[54] They who swore otherwise violated this order: "By the name of strange gods you shall not swear."[55] Although at times people swear by creatures, nevertheless, it must be known that such is the same as swearing by God. When you swear

---

[51] Jer. 4:2
[52] Wisd. of Sol. 13:1
[53] Lev. 24:16
[54] Deut. 6:13
[55] Exod. 23:13

by your soul or your head, it is as if you bind yourself to be punished by God. Thus: "But I call God to witness upon my soul."[56] And when you swear by the Gospel, you swear by God who gave the Gospel. But they sin who swear either by God or by the Gospel for any trivial reason.

2. To sanctify, we may take God's name justly. Thus, Baptism sanctifies, as St. Paul says: "But you are washed, you are sanctified, and you are justified in the name of our Lord Jesus Christ and the Spirit of God."[57]

Baptism, however, does not have power except through the invocation of the Trinity: "But Thou, O Lord, art among us, and Thy name is called upon by us."[58]

3. To expel our Adversary, we may take God's name justly. Hence, before Baptism we renounce the Devil: "Only let us be called by Thy name; take away our reproach."[59] Wherefore, if a person returns to his sins, the name of God has been taken in vain.

4. To confess God's name, we may take it justly. "How then shall they call on Him, in whom they have not believed?"[60] And again: "Whosoever shall call upon the name of the Lord shall be saved."[61]

    a. By word of mouth, we confess God's name to show forth the glory of God: "And every one that calleth upon my name,

     [56] 2 Cor. 1:23
     [57] 1 Cor. 6:11
     [58] Jer. 14:9
     [59] Isa. 4:1
     [60] Rom. 10:14
     [61] Rom. 10:13

I have created him for my glory."[62] Accordingly, if a person says anything against the glory of God, he takes the name of God in vain.

b. By our works, we confess God's name when our actions show forth His glory: "That they may see your good works and may glorify your Father who is in Heaven."[63] "Through you the name of God is blasphemed among the Gentiles."[64]

5. To defend ourselves, we take God's name justly. "The name of the Lord is a strong tower; the just runneth to it and shall be exalted."[65] "In my name they shall cast out devils."[66] "There is no other name under heaven given to men, whereby we must be saved."[67]

6. To make our works complete, we take God's name justly. Thus says the Apostle: "Whatsoever you do in word or work, do it in the name of the Lord Jesus Christ."[68] The reason is because "our help is in the name of the Lord."[69]

Sometimes it happens that a person begins a work imprudently by starting with a vow, for instance, and then does not complete either the work or the vow. And this, again, is taking God's name in vain. "If thou hast vowed anything to God, defer not to pay it."[70] "Vow and pay to the Lord your God; all ye that

---

[62] Isa. 43:7
[63] Matt. 5:16
[64] Rom. 2:24
[65] Prov. 18:10
[66] Mark 16:17
[67] Acts 4:12
[68] Col. 3:17
[69] Ps. 123:8 (RSV: Ps. 124:8)
[70] Eccles. 5:3

are round about Him bring presents."[71] "For an unfaithful and foolish promise displeaseth Him."[72]

[71]Ps. 75:12 (RSV: Ps. 76:11)
[72]Eccles. 5:3

III

THE THIRD COMMANDMENT

Remember that you keep holy the Sabbath day.

This is the Third Commandment of the Law, and very suitably is it so. For we are first commanded to adore God in our hearts and to worship one God: *Thou shalt not have strange gods before Me*. The Second Commandment tells us to revere God in our words: *Thou shalt not take the name of the Lord thy God in vain*. And the Third commands us to revere God in our actions: *Remember that thou keep holy the Sabbath day.*[73] God wished that a certain day be set aside for men to direct their minds to the service of the Lord.

A. Reasons for this Commandment

1. To put aside errors, we are told to keep holy the Sabbath.

a. The error of those who deny the first creation
The Holy Spirit saw that in the future some men would say that the world had always existed. "In the last days there shall come deceitful scoffers, walking after their own lusts, saying: 'Where is His promise or His coming? For since the time that the fathers slept, all things continue as they were from the

---

[73] Cf. St. Thomas Aquinas, *Summa Theologiae*, I-II, Q. 102, art. 4, and II-II, Q. 122, art.4

17

beginning of creation.' For of this they are willfully ignorant, that the heavens existed long ago and the earth was formed out of water and through water by the word of God."[74] God, therefore, wished that one day should be set aside in memory of the fact that He created all things in six days and that on the seventh day He rested from the creation of new creatures. This is why the Lord placed this Commandment in the Law, saying: *Remember that thou keep holy the Sabbath day.*

b. The error of those who deny the second creation
The Jews kept holy the Sabbath in memory of the first creation, but Christ at His coming brought about a new creation. For by the first creation an earthly man was created and by the second a heavenly man was formed: "For in Christ Jesus neither circumcision availeth any thing, nor uncircumcision, but a new creature."[75] This new creation is through grace, which came by the Resurrection: "That as Christ is risen from the dead by the glory of the Father, so we also may walk in newness of life. For if we have been planted together in the likeness of His death, so shall we also be in the likeness of His Resurrection."[76] And thus, because the Resurrection took place on Sunday, we celebrate that day, even as the Jews observed the Sabbath on account of the first creation.

2. To instruct us in our faith in the Redeemer, we are commanded to keep holy the Sabbath. For the flesh of Christ was not corrupted in the sepulcher, and thus it is said: "Moreover my flesh also shall rest in hope."[77] "Nor wilt Thou give Thy holy one to

---

[74] 2 Pet. 3:3-5
[75] Gal. 6:15
[76] Rom. 6:4-5
[77] Ps. 15:9 (RSV: Ps. 16:9)

see corruption."[78] Wherefore God wished that the Sabbath day should be observed and that just as the sacrifices of the Old Law signified the death of Christ, so should the quiet of the Sabbath signify the rest of His body in the sepulcher.

But we do not now observe these sacrifices because with the advent of the reality and the truth, figures of it must cease, just as the darkness is dispelled with the rising of the sun. Nevertheless, we keep the Saturdays in veneration of the Blessed Virgin, in whom remained a firm faith on that Saturday while Christ was dead.

3. To strengthen the promise of rest and to foreshadow its fulfillment, we are commanded to keep holy the Sabbath. For rest indeed was promised to us: "And it shall come to pass on that day, that God shall give thee rest from thy labor, from thy vexation, and from the hard bondage wherewith thou didst serve before."[79] "My people shall sit in the beauty of peace, in the tabernacle of confidence, and in wealthy rest."[80]

We hope for rest from three things: from the labors of the present life, from the struggles of temptations, and from servitude to the Devil. Christ promised this rest to all those who will come to Him: "Come to me, all ye that labor and are burdened, and I will refresh you. Take up my yoke and learn of me, because I am meek and humble of heart; and you shall find rest to your souls. For my yoke is sweet and my burden light."[81]

However, as we know, the Lord worked for six days and on the seventh He rested, because it is necessary in order to do a perfect work: "Behold with your eyes how I have labored a little

---

[78] Ps. 15:10 (RSV: Ps. 16:10)
[79] Isa. 14:3
[80] Isa. 32:18
[81] Matt. 11:28-30

and have found much rest to myself."[82] For the period of eternity exceeds the present time incomparably more than a thousand years exceeds one day.

4. To increase our love, we are commanded to keep holy the Sabbath. "For the corruptible body is a load upon the soul."[83] And man always tends downwards toward earthly things unless he takes means to raise himself above them. It is indeed necessary to have a certain time for this.

In fact, some do this continually: "I will bless the Lord at all times; His praise shall be ever in my mouth."[84] And again: "Pray without ceasing."[85] These shall enjoy the everlasting Sabbath.

There are others who do this (i.e., awaken love for God) during a certain portion of the day: "Seven times a day I have given praise to Thee."[86]

And some, in order to avoid being entirely apart from God, find it necessary to have a fixed day [for worship], lest they become too lukewarm in their love of God: "If you call the Sabbath delightful . . . then shalt thou be delighted in the Lord."[87] Again: "Then shalt thou abound in delights of the Almighty and shalt lift up thy face to God."[88] And accordingly this day is not set aside for the sole exercise of games, but to praise and pray to the Lord God. Wherefore St. Augustine says that it is a lesser evil to plow than to play on this day.[89]

---

[82] Ecclus. 51:35 (RSV: Sir. 51:27)
[83] Wisd. of Sol. 9:15
[84] Ps. 33:1 (RSV: Ps. 34:1)
[85] 1 Thess. 5:17
[86] Ps. 118:164 (RSV: Ps. 119:164)
[87] Isa. 58:13-14
[88] Job 22:26
[89] This is a reference to the great public spectacles and games.

5. To exercise works of kindliness to those who are subject to us, we are commanded to keep holy the Sabbath. For some are so cruel to themselves and to others that they labor ceaselessly on account of money. This is true especially of the Jews, who are most avaricious.[90] "Observe the day of the Sabbath to sanctify it . . . that thy manservant and thy maidservant may rest, even as thyself."[91]

This Commandment, therefore, was given for all of the above reasons.

B. How to keep the Sabbath holy
Remember that you keep holy (sanctify) the Sabbath day. We have already said that as the Jews celebrated the Sabbath, so do we Christians observe Sunday and all principal feasts. Let us now see the way in which we should keep these days.

1. The meanings of *holy*
We ought to know that God did not simply say to "keep" the Sabbath, but to remember to "keep it *holy*." The word *holy* may be taken in two ways:

a. Holy signifies "pure"
Sometimes *holy* (or *sanctified*) is the same as "pure": "You are washed; you are sanctified"[92] (i.e., "you are made holy").

---

[90] Our editorial obligation is to present a faithful edition of this work rather than to delete remarks that may be objectionable. We do, however, recommend a prayerful reading of the Church's numerous official documents on the attitudes that Christians are called to have toward the Jews.—*Ed.*

[91] Deut. 5:12-14

[92] 1 Cor. 6:11

b. Holy signifies "consecrated"

Then again at times *holy* is said of a thing consecrated to the worship of God, as, for instance, a place, a season, vestments, and the holy vessels.

Therefore, in these two ways we ought to celebrate the feasts: purely and by giving ourselves over to divine service. Now we must consider two things regarding this Commandment: what we should avoid on a feast day and what we should do.

2. Things to avoid on the Sabbath

We ought to avoid three things. The first is servile work.

a. Servile work

1. Impermissible servile work

"Neither do ye any work; sanctify the Sabbath day."[93] And so also it is said in the Law: "You shall do no servile work therein."[94] Now servile work is bodily work, whereas "free work" (i.e., non-servile work) is done by the mind (for instance, the exercise of the intellect and such like). We also cannot be bound to do this kind of work in a servile manner.

2. Reasons that permit servile work on the Sabbath

We ought to know, however, that servile work can be done on the Sabbath for four reasons:

[93] Jer. 17:22
[94] Lev. 23:3

22

a. Necessity. For this reason, the Lord excused the disciples plucking the ears of corn on the Sabbath, as we read in St. Matthew.[95]

b. Service of the Church. We see in the same Gospel how the priests did all things necessary in the Temple on the Sabbath day.

c. The good of our neighbor. It was on the Sabbath that the Savior cured one having a withered hand and refuted the Jews who reprimanded Him by citing the example of the sheep in a pit.[96]

d. The authority of our superiors. Thus, God commanded the Jews to circumcise on the Sabbath.[97]

b. Sin

Another thing to be avoided on the Sabbath is sin: "Take heed to your souls and carry no burdens on the Sabbath day."[98] This weight and burden on the soul is sin: "My iniquities as a heavy burden are become heavy upon me."[99] Now sin is a servile work because "whosoever committeth sin is the servant of sin."[100] Therefore, when it is said, "You shall do no servile work therein,"[101] this can be understood of sin. Thus, a person violates this Commandment as often as he commits sin on the Sabbath. And so both by working and by sin God

---

[95] Matt. 12:3-8
[96] Matt. 12:11-13
[97] John 7:22-23
[98] Jer. 17:21
[99] Ps. 37:5 (RSV: Ps. 38:4)
[100] John 8:34
[101] Lev. 23:3

23

is offended. "Thy Sabbaths and other festivals I will not abide."[102] And why? "Because your assemblies are wicked. My soul hateth your new moons and your solemnities; they are become troublesome to me."[103]

c. Idleness

Idleness should also be avoided on the Sabbath, "For idleness hath taught much evil."[104] St. Jerome says: "Always do some good work and the Devil will always find you occupied."[105] Hence, it is not good for us to keep only the principal feasts if on the others we remain idle.

"The King's honor loveth judgment" (i.e., discretion).[106] Wherefore we read that certain of the Jews were in hiding and their enemies fell upon them; but they, believing that they were not able to defend themselves on the Sabbath, were overcome and killed.[107] The same thing happens to many who are idle on the feast days: "The enemies have seen her and have mocked at her Sabbaths."[108] But all such should do as those Jews did, of whom it is said: "Whosoever shall come up against us to fight on the Sabbath day, we will fight against him."[109]

3. Things to do on the Sabbath and feast days

Remember that thou keep holy the Sabbath day. We have already said that man must keep the feast days holy and that *holy* is

---

[102] Isa. 1:13
[103] Isa. 1:13-14
[104] Ecclus. 33:29 (RSV: Sir. 33:27)
[105] St. Jerome, *Epistle 125 ad Rusticum*, 11
[106] Ps. 98:4 (RSV: Ps. 99:4)
[107] 1 Macc. 2:31-38
[108] Lam. 1:7
[109] 1 Macc. 2:41

considered in two ways (namely, "pure" and "consecrated to God"). Moreover, we have indicated what things we should abstain from on these days. Now it must be shown with what we should occupy ourselves.

a. Offer sacrifice

In the Book of Numbers,[110] God commands that every day one lamb be offered in the morning and one in the evening, but on the Sabbath day the number should be doubled. This shows that on the Sabbath we should offer sacrifice to God from all that we possess: "All things are Thine, and we have given Thee what we received from Thy hand."[111]

1. Our soul as sacrifice

We should offer our soul to God, being sorry for our sins: "A sacrifice to God is an afflicted spirit."[112] And we should pray for His blessings: "Let my prayer be directed as incense in Thy sight."[113] Feast days were instituted for that spiritual joy which is the effect of prayer. Therefore on such days our prayers should be multiplied.

2. Our body as sacrifice

Secondly, we should also offer our body by mortifying it with fasting: "I beseech you therefore, brethren, by the mercy of God, that you present your bodies as a living sacrifice."[114] And we should praise God: "The sacrifice of

---

[110] Num. 28
[111] 1 Chron. 29:14
[112] Ps. 50:19 (RSV: Ps. 51:17)
[113] Ps. 140:2 (RSV: Ps. 141:2)
[114] Rom. 12:1

praise shall honor me."[115] Therefore on these days our hymns should be more numerous.

3. Our possessions as sacrifice

Thirdly, we should sacrifice our possessions by giving alms: "And do not forget to do good and to impart, for by such sacrifice God's favor is obtained."[116] These alms ought to be more than on other days since the Sabbath is a day of common joys: "Send portions to them that have not prepared for themselves, for it is the holy day of the Lord."[117]

b. Hear God's word

Our second duty on the Sabbath is to be eager to hear the word of God. This the Jews did daily: ". . . the voices of the prophets which are read every Sabbath."[118]

Therefore Christians, whose justice should be more perfect, ought to come together on the Sabbath to hear sermons and to participate in the services of the Church: "He that is of God heareth the words of God."[119]

We likewise ought to speak with profit to others: "Let no evil speech proceed from your mouth, but only that speech which is good unto sanctification."[120] These two practices are good for the soul of the sinner because they change his heart for the better: "Are not my words as a fire, saith the Lord, and as a hammer that breaketh the rock in pieces?"[121] The opposite effect is had on those, even the perfect, who neither speak

[115] Ps. 49:23 (RSV: Ps. 50:23)
[116] Heb. 13:16
[117] 2 Esd. 8:10 (RSV: Neh. 8:10)
[118] Acts 13:27
[119] John 8:47
[120] Eph. 4:29
[121] Jer. 23:29

nor hear profitable things: "Evil communications corrupt good manners. Awake, ye just, and sin not."[122] "Thy words have I hidden in my heart."[123] God's word enlightens the ignorant: "Thy word is a lamp unto my feet."[124] It inflames the lukewarm: "The word of the Lord inflamed him."[125]

c. Contemplate divine things
The contemplation of divine things may be exercised on the Sabbath. However, this is for the more perfect: "O taste, and see that the Lord is sweet."[126]

1. Rest in divine contemplation
This is for the quiet of the soul, for just as the tired body desires rest, so also does the soul. But the soul's proper rest is in God: "Be Thou unto me a God, a protector, and a house of refuge."[127] "There remaineth therefore a day of rest for the people of God. For he that is entered into his rest, the same also hath rested from his works, as God did from His."[128] "When I go into my house, I shall repose myself with her" (i.e., with Wisdom).[129]

2. Rests that precede divine contemplation
However, before the soul arrives at this rest, three other rests must precede:

---

[122] 1 Cor. 15:33-34
[123] Ps. 118:11 (RSV: Ps. 119:11)
[124] Ps. 118:105 (RSV: Ps. 119:105)
[125] Ps. 104:19 (RSV: Ps. 105:19)
[126] Ps. 33:9 (RSV: Ps. 34:8)
[127] Ps. 30:3 (RSV: Ps. 31:2)
[128] Heb. 4:9-10
[129] Wisd. of Sol. 8:16

a. Rest from the turmoil of sin: "But the wicked are like the raging sea which cannot rest."[130]

b. Rest from the passions of the flesh: "For the flesh lusteth against the spirit, and the spirit against the flesh."[131]

c. Rest from the occupations of the world: "Martha, Martha, thou art careful and art troubled about many things."[132]

3. Eternal rest

And then after all these things, the soul rests peacefully in God: "If thou call the Sabbath delightful . . . then shalt thou be delighted in the Lord."[133] The saints gave up everything to possess this rest, "for it is a pearl of great price which a man having found, hid it, and for joy thereof goeth and selleth all that he hath and buyeth that field."[134] This rest in truth is eternal life and heavenly joy: "This is my rest for ever and ever; here will I dwell, for I have chosen it."[135]

And to this rest
may the Lord bring us all!

---

[130] Isa. 57:20
[131] Gal. 5:17
[132] Luke 10:41
[133] Isa. 58:13-14
[134] Matt. 13:45-46
[135] Ps. 131:14 (RSV: Ps. 132:14)

IV

THE FOURTH COMMANDMENT
Honor thy father and thy mother, that thou mayest be
long-lived upon the land which the Lord thy God will give thee.

Perfection for man consists in the love of God and of neighbor. The three Commandments on the first tablet pertain to the love of God; the seven on the second pertain to the love of neighbor.

We must "love, not in word nor in tongue, but in deed and in truth."[136] For a man to love thus, he must avoid evil and do good. Thus, some of the Commandments prescribe good acts and others forbid evil deeds. Also, although avoiding evil is within our power, we are incapable of doing good to everyone. Thus, St. Augustine says that we should love all, but we are not bound to do good to all.

A. Reasons we should honor our parents

1. Their union with us
Among those to whom we are bound to do good are those in some way united to us. Thus, "if any man have not care of his own and especially of those of his house, he hath denied the faith."[137] Now amongst all our relatives there are none closer than our father and mother. "We ought to love God first," says

---

[136] 1 John 3:18
[137] 1 Tim. 5:8

St. Ambrose, "then our father and mother." Hence, God has given us the Commandment: *Honor thy father and thy mother.*[138]

2. The benefits they have given us

The Philosopher[139] also gives another reason for this honor to parents, in that we cannot make an equal return to our parents for the great benefits they have granted to us. Therefore, an offended parent has the right to send his son away, but the son has no such right.[140]

Parents, indeed, provide three benefits to children:

a. Being

The first is that they bring us into being: "Honor thy father and forget not the groanings of thy mother; remember that thou hadst not been born but through them."[141]

b. Nourishment and support

Second, they furnish us nourishment and the support necessary for life. For a child comes naked into the world, as Job relates,[142] but his parents provide for him.

c. Instruction

Instruction is the third benefit that parents provide children: "We have had fathers of our flesh for instructors."[143] "Hast thou children? Instruct them."[144] Parents, therefore, should give instruction without delay to their children because "a

---

[138] Cf. *Summa Theologiae*, II-II, Q. 122, art. 5; Q. 101, art. 2, 4
[139] Aristotle was known as "The Philosopher."
[140] Aristotle, *Nichomachean Ethics*, 1163b
[141] Ecclus. 7:29-30 (RSV: Sir. 7:27-28)
[142] Job 1:21
[143] Heb. 12:9
[144] Ecclus. 7:25 (RSV: Sir. 7:23)

young man according to his way, even when he is old, will not depart from it."[145] And again: "It is good for a man when he hath borne the yoke from his youth."[146] Now the instruction which Tobias gave his son was this: to fear the Lord and to abstain from sin.[147] This is indeed contrary to those parents who approve of the misdeeds of their children.

Children therefore receive from their parents birth, nourishment, and instruction.

B. Obligations to parents that arise from these benefits
In return for these benefits, we owe our parents three things:

1. Honor, because they gave us existence
Since we owe our birth to our parents, we ought to honor them more than any other superiors, because from those others we receive only temporal things: "He that feareth the Lord honoreth his parents and will serve them as his masters that brought him into the world. Honor thy father in work and word and all patience, that a blessing may come upon thee from him."[148] In doing this you shall also honor yourself because "the glory of a man is from honor of his father, and a father without honor is the disgrace of his son."[149]

2. Support, because they gave us nourishment
Since we receive nourishment from our parents in our childhood, we must support them in their old age: "Son, support the old age

---

[145]Prov. 22:6
[146]Lam. 3:27
[147]Tob. 4:5
[148]Ecclus. 3:8-10 (RSV: Sir. 3:6-8)
[149]Ecclus. 3:13 (RSV: Sir. 3:11)

of thy father and grieve him not in his life. And if his understanding fail, have patience with him and despise him not when thou art in thy strength. . . . Of what an evil fame is he that forsaketh his father! And he is cursed of God that angereth his mother."[150]

For the humiliation of those who act contrary to this, Cassiodorus relates how young storks (when their parents have lost their feathers because of approaching old age and are unable to find suitable food) make the parent storks comfortable with their own feathers and bring back food for their worn-out bodies. Thus, by this affectionate exchange the young ones repay the parents for what they received when they were young.[151]

3. Obedience, because they gave us instruction

We must obey our parents, for they have instructed us. "Children, obey your parents in all things."[152] This excepts, of course, those things which are contrary to God. St. Jerome says that the only loyalty in such cases is to be cruel.[153] "If any man hate not his father and mother . . . he cannot be my disciple."[154] This is to say that God is in the truest sense our Father: "Is not He thy Father who hath possessed thee, made thee, and created thee?"[155]

C. Rewards for honoring our parents

Honor thy father and thy mother. Among all the Commandments, this one only has the additional words: . . . *that thou mayest be long-lived upon the land.* The reason for this is lest it be thought that there is no reward for those who honor their parents, seeing that it is a

---

[150] Ecclus. 3:14-15,18 (RSV: Sir. 3:12-13,16)
[151] Cassiodorus, *Variarum*, Lib. 2, Ep. 14
[152] Col. 3:20
[153] St. Jerome, *Epistle 14 ad Heliodorum*, 2-3
[154] Luke 14:26
[155] Deut. 32:6

natural obligation. Hence it must be known that five most desirable rewards are promised to those who honor their parents.

1. Grace and glory

The first reward is grace for the present life and glory in the life to come, which surely are greatly to be desired: "Honor thy father . . . that a blessing may come upon thee from him and his blessing may remain in the end."[156]

The very opposite comes upon those who dishonor their parents. Indeed, they are cursed in the Law by God.[157] It is also written: "He that is unjust in that which is little is unjust also in that which is greater."[158]

But this our natural life is as nothing compared with the life of grace. And so, therefore, if you do not acknowledge the blessing of the natural life which you owe to your parents, then you are unworthy of the life of grace, which is greater, and all the more unworthy of the life of glory, which is the greatest of all blessings.

2. A long life

The second reward is a long life: . . . *that thou mayest be long-lived upon the land*. For "he that honoreth his father shall enjoy a long life."[159]

Now this means a long life which is a full life; and it is not observed in time but in activity, as the Philosopher observes. Life, however, is full inasmuch as it is a life of virtue. So a man who is virtuous and holy enjoys a long life even if in body he dies young: "Being perfect in a short space, he fulfilled a long time — for his

---

[156]Ecclus. 3:9-10 (RSV: Sir. 3:8-9)
[157]Deut. 27:16
[158]Luke 16:10
[159]Ecclus. 3:7 (RSV: Sir. 3:6)

soul pleased God."[160] Thus, for example, he is a good merchant who does as much business in one day as another would do in a year. And note well that it sometimes happens that a temporally long life may lead up to a spiritual as well as a bodily death, as was the case with Judas.

The reward for keeping this Commandment is a long life for the body. The very opposite (death) is the fate of those who dishonor their parents. We receive our life from them; and just as soldiers owe fealty to the king and lose their rights in case of any treachery, so also they who dishonor their parents deserve to forfeit their lives: "The eye that mocketh at his father and that despiseth the labor of his mother in bearing him, let the ravens pick it out and the young eagles eat it."[161] Here the *ravens* signify officials of kings and princes, who in turn are the *young eagles*.

But if it happens that such are not bodily punished, they nevertheless cannot escape the death of the soul. It is not well, therefore, for a father to give too much power to his children: "Give not to son or wife, brother or friend, power over thee while thou livest; and give not thy estate to another, lest thou repent."[162]

3. Grateful and pleasing children

The third reward is to have in turn grateful and pleasing children. For a father naturally treasures his children, but the contrary is not always the case: "He that honoreth his father shall have joy in his own children."[163] Again: "With what measure you measure, it shall be measured to you again."[164]

---

[160] Wisd. of Sol. 4:13-14
[161] Prov. 30:17
[162] Ecclus. 33:20 (RSV: Sir. 33:19)
[163] Ecclus. 3:6 (RSV: Sir. 3:5)
[164] Matt. 7:2

4. A praiseworthy reputation

The fourth reward is a praiseworthy reputation: "For the glory of a man is from the honor of his father."[165] And again: "Of what an evil fame is he that forsaketh his father?"[166]

5. Riches

A fifth reward is riches: "The father's blessing establisheth the houses of his children, but the mother's curse rooteth up the foundation."[167]

D. Others who deserve the reverence due to fathers

Honor thy father and thy mother. A man is called father not only by reason of generation but also for other reasons, and to each of these there is due a certain reverence.

1. The Apostles and saints are called *fathers* because of their doctrine and their exemplification of faith: "Although you have ten thousand instructors in Christ, yet you have not many fathers. For in Christ Jesus, by the gospel, I have begotten you."[168] And again: "Let us now praise men of renown and our fathers in their generation."[169] However, let us praise them not in word only but by imitating them. And we do this if nothing is found in us contrary to what we praise in them.

2. Our superiors in the Church are also called *fathers*. They, too, are to be respected as the ministers of God: "Remember your prelates . . . ; consider the outcome of their life and imitate their

---

[165] Ecclus. 3:13 (RSV: Sir. 3:11)
[166] Ecclus. 3:18 (RSV: Sir. 3:16)
[167] Ecclus. 3:11 (RSV: Sir. 3:9)
[168] 1 Cor. 4:15
[169] Ecclus. 44:1 (RSV: Sir. 44:1)

faith."[170] And again: "He that heareth you, heareth me; and he that despiseth you, despiseth me."[171] We honor our prelates by showing them obedience ("Obey your prelates, and be subject to them")[172] and also by paying them tithes: "Honor the Lord with thy substance and give Him of the first of thy fruits."[173]

3. Rulers and kings are called *fathers:* "Father, if the prophet had bid thee do some great thing, surely thou shouldst have done it."[174] We call them fathers because their whole care is the good of their people. And we honor them by being subject to them: "Let every soul be subject to the governing authorities."[175] We should be subject to them not merely through fear, but through love; and not merely because it is reasonable, but because of the dictates of our conscience, because "there is no authority but from God."[176] And so to all such must we render what is due to them: "Tribute, to whom tribute is due; custom, to whom custom; fear, to whom fear; and honor, to whom honor."[177] And again: "My son, fear the Lord and the king."[178]

4. Our benefactors are also called *fathers:* "Be merciful to the fatherless as a father."[179] He, too, [who gives his bond] is like a father, of whom it is said: "Forget not the kindness of thy surety."[180] On the other hand, the ungrateful shall receive a

---

[170] Heb. 13:7
[171] Luke 10:16
[172] Heb. 13:17
[173] Prov. 3:9
[174] 4 Kings 5:13 (RSV: 2 Kings 5:13)
[175] Rom. 13:1
[176] Ibid.
[177] Rom. 13:7
[178] Prov. 24:21
[179] Ecclus. 4:10 (RSV: Sir. 4:10)
[180] Ecclus. 29:19 (RSV: Sir. 29:15)

punishment such as is written: "The hope of the ungrateful shall melt away as the winter's ice."[181]

5. Old men also are called *fathers:* "Ask thy father and he will declare to thee; thy elders and they will tell thee."[182] And again: "Rise up before the hoary head and honor the person of the aged man."[183] "In the company of great men take not upon thee to speak; and when the ancients are present, speak not much."[184] "Hear in silence, and for thy reverence good grace shall come to thee."[185]

Now all these fathers must be honored because they all resemble to some degree our Father who is in Heaven. And of all of them it is said: "He that despiseth you, despiseth me."[186]

---

[181] Wisd. of Sol. 16:29
[182] Deut. 32:7
[183] Lev. 19:32
[184] Ecclus. 32:13 (RSV: Sir. 32:9)
[185] Ecclus. 32:9 (No equivalent in RSV)
[186] Luke 10:16

V

THE FIFTH COMMANDMENT
Thou shalt not kill.

In the divine law which tells us we must love God and our neighbor, it is commanded that we not only do good but also avoid evil. The greatest evil that can be done to one's neighbor is to take his life. This is prohibited in the Commandment: *Thou shalt not kill.*[187]

A. Killing

1. Errors regarding killing
In connection with this Commandment there are errors regarding the killing of animals, the execution of criminals, and suicide.

a. The killing of animals
Some have said that it is not permitted to kill even brute animals. But this is false, because it is not a sin to use that which is subordinate to the power of man. It is in the natural order that plants nourish animals, certain animals nourish others, and all nourish man: "Even as the green herbs have I delivered them all to you."[188] The Philosopher says that

---

[187]Cf. Aquinas, *Summa Theologiae*, II-II, Q. 69, art. 2, 3; and Q. 112, art. 6
[188]Gen. 9:3

hunting is like a just war.[189] And St. Paul says: "Whatsoever is sold in the meat market eat, asking no questions for conscience' sake."[190] Therefore, the sense of the Commandment is: "Thou shalt not kill *men*."

b. The execution of criminals

Some have held that the killing of man is prohibited altogether. They believe that judges in the civil courts are murderers when they condemn men to death according to the laws.

Against this St. Augustine says that God by this Commandment does not take away from Himself the right to kill. Thus, we read: "I will kill and I will make to live."[191] It is, therefore, lawful for a judge to kill according to a mandate from God, since in this act God operates and every law is a command of God: "By me kings reign and lawgivers decree just things."[192] And again: "For if thou dost that which is evil, fear; for he beareth not the sword in vain, because he is God's minister...."[193] To Moses also was it said: "Wizards thou shalt not suffer to live."[194] Thus that which is lawful to God is lawful for His ministers when they act by His mandate.

It is evident that God, who is the author of laws, has every right to inflict death on account of sin. For "the wages of sin is death."[195] Neither does His minister sin in inflicting that punishment. The sense, therefore, of *Thou shalt not kill* is that one shall not kill by one's own authority.

[189] Aristotle, *Politics*, 1256b
[190] 1 Cor. 10:25
[191] Deut. 32:39
[192] Prov. 8:15
[193] Rom. 13:4
[194] Exod. 22:18
[195] Rom. 6:23

c. Suicide

There are those who held that although this Commandment forbids a person to kill another person, yet it is lawful to kill oneself. Thus, there are the examples of Samson[196] and Cato and certain virgins who threw themselves into the flames, as St. Augustine relates in *The City of God*.[197] But he also explains this in the words: "He who kills himself certainly kills a man."[198]

If it is not lawful to kill except by the authority of God, then it is not lawful to kill oneself except either upon the authority of God or instructed by the Holy Spirit, as was the case of Samson. Therefore: *Thou shalt not kill*.

2. Ways of killing a man's body

One may kill a man in several ways.

a. By one's own hand: "Your hands are full of blood."[199] This is not only against charity, which tells us to love our neighbor as ourself: "No murderer hath eternal life abiding in himself."[200] But it is also against nature, for "every beast loveth its like."[201] And so it is said: "He that striketh a man with a will to kill him, shall be put to death."[202] He who does this is more cruel than the wolf, of which Aristotle says that one wolf will not eat of the flesh of another wolf.[203]

---

[196] Judg. 16
[197] St. Augustine, *City of God*, 1.27
[198] Ibid.
[199] Isa. 1:15
[200] 1 John 3:15
[201] Ecclus. 13:19 (RSV: Sir. 13:15)
[202] Exod. 21:12
[203] Aristotle, *De Historia Animalium*, 571b

b. By word of mouth, we can kill by giving counsel to anyone against another by provocation, accusation, or detraction: "... the sons of men whose teeth are weapons and arrows, and their tongue a sharp sword."[204]

c. By helping another kill, we can kill, as it is written: "My son, walk not thou with them . . . for their feet run to evil, and they make haste to shed blood."[205]

d. By consenting to another's death, we can kill: "They who do such things are worthy of death; and not only they that do them, but also they that consent to them that do them."[206]

e. By not preventing another's death, we can kill: "Deliver them that are led to death."[207] If we can prevent it, yet do not do so through negligence or avarice, we also kill. Thus, St. Ambrose says: "Give food to him that is dying of hunger; if you do not, you are his murderer."

3. Ways of killing a man's soul

We have already considered the killing of the body, but some also kill the soul by drawing it away from the life of grace, specifically by inducing it to commit mortal sin: "He was a murderer from the beginning"[208] (i.e., insofar as he drew men into sin).

4. Ways of killing both body and soul

Others, however, slay both body and soul, and in two ways:

---

[204] Ps. 56:5 (RSV: Ps. 57:4)
[205] Prov. 1:15-16
[206] Rom. 1:32
[207] Prov. 24:11
[208] John 8:44

a. By the murder of one with child, whereby the child is killed both in body and soul.

b. By committing suicide

B. Anger

In the Gospel of St. Matthew[209] Christ taught that our justice should be greater than the justice of the Old Law. This means that Christians should observe the Commandments of the Law more perfectly than the Jews observed them. The reason is that greater effort deserves a better reward: "He who soweth sparingly, shall also reap sparingly."[210] The Old Law promised a temporary and earthly reward: "If you be willing and will hearken to Me, you shall eat the good things of the land."[211] But in the New Law heavenly and eternal things are promised. Therefore, justice, which is the observance of the Commandments, should be more generous among Christians because they expect a greater reward.

1. Anger and killing

The Lord specifically mentioned this Commandment when He said: "You have heard that it was said to them of old: *Thou shalt not kill*. . . . But I say to you that anyone who is angry with his brother shall be in danger of the judgment."[212] By this is meant the penalty which the Law prescribes: "If a man kill his neighbor on set purpose and by lying in wait for him, . . . take him away from my altar, that he may die."[213]

[209] Matt. 5:17-48
[210] 2 Cor. 9:6
[211] Isa.1:19
[212] Matt. 5:21-22
[213] Exod. 21:14

2. Obligations regarding anger

a. Be not quickly provoked to anger

"Let men be swift to hear, but slow to speak and slow to anger."[214] There are two reasons for this.

1. Anger is virtuous only sometimes

a. The wise man is properly subject to moderate anger

Anger is a sin punished by God, but is all anger contrary to virtue? There are two opinions about this. The Stoics said that the wise man is free from all passions. Even more, they maintained that true virtue consists in perfect quiet of soul. The Peripatetics, on the other hand, held that the wise man is subject to anger but in a moderate degree. This is the more accurate opinion.

1. Christ was angry sometimes

It is first proven by authority, for the Gospel shows that these passions were attributed to Christ in whom was the full fountainhead of wisdom.

2. Anger sometimes has a good purpose

Secondly, it is proven from reason. If all the passions were opposed to virtue, then there would be some powers of the soul which would be without good purpose. Indeed, they would be positively harmful to man, since they would have no acts in keeping with them. Thus, the irascible and concupiscible powers would be given to man to no purpose.

---

[214]James 1:19

It must therefore be concluded that sometimes anger is virtuous and sometimes it is not.

b. The kinds of anger

We see this if we consider anger in three different ways.

1. Anger can be a judgment of reason

First, we find anger as it exists solely in the judgment of reason, without any perturbation of soul. This is more properly not anger but judgment. Thus, the Lord punishing the wicked is said to be angry: "I will bear the wrath of the Lord because I have sinned against Him."[215]

2. Righteous anger

Anger is considered a passion. This is in the sensitive appetite and is twofold. Sometimes it is ordered by reason or restrained within proper limits by reason, as when a person is angry because it is justly fitting to be angry and within proper limits. This is an act of virtue and is called *righteous anger*. Thus, the Philosopher says that meekness is not opposed to anger. This kind of anger, then, is not a sin.

3. Sinful anger

Anger which overthrows the judgment of reason is always sinful, sometimes mortally and sometimes venially. And whether it is one or the other will depend on that object to which the anger incites, which is sometimes mortal, sometimes venial.

---

[215] Mic. 7:9

45

a. Mortally sinful anger

Sin may be mortal in two ways: either in its *genus* or by reason of its circumstances. For example, murder would seem to be a mortal sin in its *genus* because it is directly opposite to a divine Commandment.

Thus, consent to murder is a mortal sin in its *genus* because if an act itself is a mortal sin, then consent to the act will be also a mortal sin.

b. Venially sinful anger

Sometimes, however, an act itself is mortal in its *genus* but, nevertheless, the impulse is not mortal because it is without consent. This is the same as when one is moved by the impulse of concupiscence to fornication and yet does not consent: here one does not commit a sin.

The same holds true of anger. For anger is really the impulse to avenge an injury which one has suffered. Now, if this impulse of the passion is so great that reason is weakened, then it is a mortal sin.

On the other hand, if up to the moment of consent the reason is not perverted by the passion (and if consent is given without any perversion of the reason), then there is no mortal sin.

"Whosoever is angry with his brother, shall be in danger of the judgment."[216] This must be understood of that impulse of passion tending to

[216] Mt. 5:21

46

do injury to the extent that reason is perverted. This impulse, inasmuch as it is consented to, is a mortal sin.

2. Anger diminishes freedom

The second reason we should not be easily provoked to anger is that every man loves liberty and hates restraint. But he who is filled with anger is not master of himself: "Who can bear the violence of one provoked?"[217] And again: "A stone is heavy and sand weighty, but the anger of a fool is heavier than both."[218]

b. Do not remain angry long

We should also take care that we do not remain angry very long: "Be ye angry and sin not."[219] And: "Let not the sun go down upon your anger."[220] The reason for this is given in the Gospel by our Lord: "Be at agreement with thy adversary betimes whilst thou art in the way with him, lest perhaps thy adversary deliver thee to the judge, the judge deliver thee to the officer, and thou be cast into prison. Amen, I say unto thee, thou shalt not go out from hence till thou repay the last farthing."[221]

c. Control the intensity of your anger

We should beware lest our anger grow in intensity, having its beginning in the heart and finally leading on to hatred. For there is this difference between anger and hatred, that anger

---

[217] Prov. 27:4
[218] Prov. 27:3
[219] Ps. 4:5 (RSV: Ps. 4:4)
[220] Eph. 4:26
[221] Matt. 5:25-26

is sudden but hatred is long-lived and, thus, is a mortal sin: "Whosoever hateth his brother is a murderer."[222] And the reason is that he kills both himself (by destroying charity) and another. Thus, St. Augustine in his *Rule* says: "Let there be no quarrels among you; or if they do arise, then let them end quickly, lest anger should grow into hatred, the mote become a beam, and the soul become a murderer."[223] Again: "A passionate man stirreth up strifes."[224] "Cursed be their fury because it was stubborn, and their wrath because it was cruel."[225]

d. Do not let wrath explode in angry words

We must take care lest our wrath explode in angry words: "A fool immediately showeth his anger."[226] Now angry words are twofold in effect: either they injure another or they express one's own pride in oneself. Our Lord referred to the first when He said, "And whosoever shall say to his brother, 'Thou fool,' shall be in danger of hellfire."[227] And He referred to the latter in the words: "And he that shall say, 'Raca,' shall be in danger of the council."[228] Moreover: "A mild answer breaketh wrath, but a harsh word stirreth up fury."[229]

e. Do not let anger lead to evil deeds

Finally, we must beware lest anger provoke us to deeds. In all our dealings we should observe two things: justice and mercy.

[222] 1 John 3:15
[223] St. Augustine, *Epistle*, 211, 14
[224] Prov. 15:18
[225] Gen. 49:7
[226] Prov. 12:16
[227] Matt. 5:22
[228] Ibid.
[229] Prov. 15:1

But anger hinders us in both: "For the anger of a man worketh not the justice of God."[230] Such a one may indeed be willing, but his anger prevents him. A certain philosopher once said to a man who had offended him: "I would punish you, were I not angry." "Anger hath no mercy, nor fury when it breaketh forth."[231] "In their fury they slew a man."[232]

It is for all this that Christ taught us not only to beware of murder but also of anger. The good physician removes the external symptoms of a malady. Furthermore, he even removes the very root of the illness so that there will be no relapse. So, also, the Lord wishes us to avoid the beginnings of sins. Thus, anger should be avoided because it is the beginning of murder.

[230] James 1:20
[231] Prov. 27:4
[232] Gen. 49:6

VI

THE SIXTH COMMANDMENT
Thou shalt not commit adultery.

A. Adultery

After the prohibition of murder, adultery is forbidden. This is fitting, since husband and wife are as one body. "They shall be," says the Lord, "two in one flesh."[233]

Therefore, after an injury inflicted upon a man in his own person, none is so grave as that which is inflicted upon a person with whom he is joined.[234] Adultery is forbidden both to the wife and the husband.

1. Adultery of the wife

We shall consider first the adultery of the wife, since in this seems to lie the greater sin. For a wife who commits adultery is guilty of three grave sins which are implied in the following words: "So every woman that leaveth her husband, . . . first, she hath been unfaithful to the Law of the Most High; second, she hath offended against her husband; and third, she hath fornicated in adultery and hath gotten her children of another man."[235]

---

[233]Gen. 2:24
[234]Cf. Aquinas, *Summa Theologiae*, II-II, Q. 122, art. 6; Q. 154
[235]Ecclus. 23:32-33 (RSV: Sir. 23:22-23)

a. Infidelity to the Law of God

First, therefore, the adulteress has sinned by lack of faith, since she is unfaithful to the Law wherein God has forbidden adultery. Moreover, she has spurned the ordinance of God: "What therefore God has joined together, let no man put asunder."[236] Also she has sinned against the institution or sacrament, because marriage is contracted before the eyes of the Church and thereupon God is called, as it were, to witness a bond of fidelity which must be kept: "The Lord hath been witness between thee and the wife of thy youth whom thou hast despised."[237] Therefore, she has sinned against the Law of God, against a precept of the Church, and against a sacrament of God.

b. Infidelity to her husband

Secondly, the adulteress sins by infidelity because she has betrayed her husband: "The wife hath not power of her own body, but the husband."[238] In fact, without the consent of the husband she cannot observe celibacy. If adultery is committed, then, an act of treachery is perpetrated in that the wife gives herself to another, just as if a servant gave himself to another master: "She forsaketh the guide of her youth and hath forgotten the covenant of her God."[239]

c. Theft

Thirdly, the adulteress commits the sin of theft in that she brings forth children from a man not her husband. This is a most grave theft in that she expends her heredity upon

[236] Matt. 19:6
[237] Mal. 2:14
[238] 1 Cor. 7:4
[239] Prov. 2:17-18

children not her husband's. Let it be noted that such a one should encourage her children to enter religion or upon such a walk of life that they do not succeed in the property of her husband. Therefore, an adulteress is guilty of sacrilege, treachery, and theft.

2. Adultery of the husband

Husbands, however, do not sin any less than wives, although they sometimes may salve themselves to the contrary. This is clear for three reasons.

a. Violation of the equality of rights between spouses

First, adultery is a sin because it violates the equality which holds between husband and wife, for "the husband also hath not power of his own body, but the wife."[240] Therefore, as far as the rights of matrimony are concerned, one cannot act without the consent of the other. As an indication of this, God did not form woman from the foot or from the head, but from the rib of the man.

Now marriage was at no time a perfect state until the law of Christ came, because a Jewish husband could have many wives, but a Jewish wife could not have many husbands. Hence, equality did not exist.

b. Defect of strength

Secondly, adultery is a sin because strength is a special quality of the man, while the passion proper to the woman is concupiscence: "Ye husbands, likewise dwelling with them according to knowledge, giving honor to the female as to the weaker

---

[240] 1 Cor. 7:4

vessel."[241] Therefore, if you ask from your wife what you do not keep yourself, then you are unfaithful.

c. Undermining the authority of the husband

Thirdly, adultery is a sin because of the authority of the husband. For the husband is head of the wife and, as is said, "Women may not speak in the church. . . . If they would learn anything, let them ask their husbands at home."[242] The husband is the teacher of his wife. God, therefore, gave the Commandment to the husband.

Now as regards fulfillment of their duties, a priest who fails is more guilty than a layman and a bishop more than a priest, because it is especially incumbent upon them to teach others. In like manner, the husband who commits adultery breaks faith by not obeying that which he ought. Thus, God forbids adultery both to men and women.

B. Fornication and impurity

Now it must be known that although some believe that adultery is a sin, yet they do not believe that simple fornication is a mortal sin. Against them stand the words of St. Paul: "For fornicators and adulterers God will judge."[243] "Do not err: neither fornicators . . . nor adulterers, nor the effeminate, nor those who lie shall possess the kingdom of God."[244] Since only mortal sin excludes us from the kingdom of God, fornication must be a mortal sin.

But one might say that there is no reason why fornication should be a mortal sin since the body of the wife is not given, as in adultery. I say, however, if the body of the wife is not given, nevertheless,

---

[241] 1 Pet. 3:7
[242] 1 Cor. 14:34-35
[243] Heb. 13:4
[244] 1 Cor. 6:9

there is given the body of Christ which was given to the husband when he was sanctified in Baptism.

If, then, a husband must not betray his wife, with much more reason must he not be unfaithful to Christ: "Know you not that your bodies are the members of Christ? Shall I then take the members of Christ and make them the members of a harlot? God forbid!"[245] It is heretical to say that fornication is not a mortal sin.

Moreover, it must be known that this Commandment does not merely forbid adultery but also every form of immodesty and impurity.

C. Married intercourse

There are some who say that intercourse between married persons is not devoid of sin. But this is heretical, for the Apostle says: "Let marriage be honorable in all and the bed undefiled."[246] Not only is it devoid of sin but, for those in the state of grace, it is meritorious for eternal life. Sometimes, however, it may be a venial sin and sometimes a mortal sin.

1. For procreation: When it is had with the intention of bringing forth offspring, married intercourse is an act of virtue.

2. For mutual comfort: When it is had with the intent of rendering mutual comfort, married intercourse is an act of justice.

3. For the excitement of lust: When it is a cause of exciting lust, although within the limits of marriage, married intercourse is a venial sin.

---

[245] 1 Cor. 6:15
[246] Heb. 13:4

4. For illicit ends: When married intercourse goes beyond these limits so as to intend intercourse with another, if possible, it is a mortal sin.

D. The prohibition of adultery and fornication
Adultery and fornication are forbidden for a number of reasons.

1. They destroy the soul
First, adultery and fornication are forbidden because they destroy the soul: "He that is an adulterer shall destroy his own soul through the folly of his heart."[247] It says *through the folly of his heart,* which means "whenever the flesh dominates the spirit."

2. They destroy life
Secondly, adultery and fornication deprive one of life, for one guilty of such should die according to the Law, as we read in Leviticus[248] and Deuteronomy.[249] Sometimes the guilty one is not punished bodily in this life, which is to his disadvantage since punishment of the body may be borne with patience and is conducive to the remission of sins. Nevertheless, he shall be punished in the future life.

3. They waste substance
Thirdly, adultery and fornication consume a person's substance, just as happened to the prodigal son in that "he wasted his substance living riotously."[250] "Give not thy soul to harlots in any way, lest thou destroy thyself and thy inheritance."[251]

---

[247] Prov. 6:32
[248] Lev. 20:10
[249] Deut. 22:22
[250] Luke 15:13
[251] Ecclus. 9:6 (RSV: Sir. 9:6)

4. They defile offspring

Fourthly, adultery and fornication defile offspring: "The children of adulterers shall not come to perfection and the seed of the unlawful bed shall be rooted out. And if they live long they shall be nothing regarded and their last old age shall be without honor."[252] And again: "Otherwise your children should be unclean, but now they are holy."[253] Thus, they are never honored in the Church, but if they be clerics their dishonor may go without shame.

5. They destroy honor

Fifthly, adultery and fornication take away one's honor and this especially is applicable to women: "Every woman that is a harlot shall be trodden upon as dung in the way."[254] And of the husband it is said: "He gathereth to himself shame and dishonor, and his reproach shall not be blotted out."[255]

St. Gregory says that sins of the flesh are more shameful and less blameful than those of the spirit, and the reason is because they are common to the beasts. "Man when he was in honor did not understand; and he hath been compared to senseless beasts, and made like to them."[256]

---

[252]Wisd. of Sol. 3:16-17
[253]1 Cor. 7:14
[254]Ecclus. 9:10 (No equivalent in RSV)
[255]Prov. 6:33
[256]Ps. 48:21 (RSV: Ps. 49:20)

VII

THE SEVENTH COMMANDMENT
Thou shalt not steal.

In the Commandments, the Lord specifically forbids injury to our neighbor. Thus, *Thou shalt not kill* forbids us to injure our neighbor in his own person; *Thou shalt not commit adultery* forbids injury to the person to whom one is bound in marriage; and now the Commandment, *Thou shalt not steal*, forbids us to injure our neighbor in his goods. This Commandment forbids us to take wrongfully any worldly goods whatsoever.[257]

A. Ways of stealing
Theft can be committed in a number of ways:

1. By taking stealthily, theft can be committed: "If the householder had known the hour that the thief would come. . . ."[258] Stealing is an act wholly blameworthy because it is a form of treachery. "Shame . . . is upon the thief."[259]

2. By taking with violence, theft can likewise be committed. This is even a greater injury: "They have violently robbed the

---

[257]Cf. Aquinas, *Summa Theologiae*, II-II, Q. 122, Art. 6
[258]Matt. 24:43
[259]Ecclus. 5:17 (RSV: Sir. 5:14)

fatherless."[260] Among those who do such things are wicked kings and rulers: "Her princes are in the midst of her as roaring lions; her judges are evening wolves who have left nothing for the morning."[261] They act contrary to the will of God, who wishes a rule according to justice: "By me kings reign and lawgivers decree just things."[262] Sometimes they do such things stealthily and sometimes with violence: "Thy princes are faithless companions of thieves. They all love bribes; they run after rewards."[263] At times they steal by enacting laws and enforcing them for profit only: "Woe to them that make wicked laws."[264] And St. Augustine says that every wrongful usurpation is theft when he asks: "What are thrones but forms of thievery?"[265]

3. By not paying wages that are due, theft can be committed: "The wages of him that hath been hired by thee shall not abide by thee until the morning."[266] This means that a man must pay every one his due, whether he be prince, prelate, or cleric: "Render therefore to all men their dues: tribute, to whom tribute is due; custom, to whom custom."[267] Hence, we are bound to give a return to rulers who guard our safety.

4. By fraudulent buying and selling, theft can be committed: "Thou shalt not have diverse weights in thy bag, a greater and a lesser."[268] And again: "Do not any unjust thing in judgment, in

---

[260] Job 24:9
[261] Soph. 3:3 (RSV: Zeph. 3:3)
[262] Prov. 8:15
[263] Isa. 1:23
[264] Isa. 10:1
[265] St. Augustine, *The City of God,* 4.4
[266] Lev. 19:13
[267] Rom. 13:7
[268] Deut. 25:13

rule, in weight, or in measure."[269] All this is directed against the keepers of wineshops who mix water with the wine. Usury is also forbidden: "Who shall dwell in Thy tabernacle or who shall rest in Thy holy hill? . . . He that hath not put his money out to usury."[270] This is also against money-changers who commit many frauds and against the sellers of cloth and other goods.

5. By buying promotions to positions of temporal or spiritual honor, theft can be committed. "The riches which he hath swallowed, he shall vomit up; and God shall draw them out of his belly,"[271] has reference to temporal position. Thus, all tyrants who hold by force a kingdom, province, or land are thieves and are held to restitution. Concerning spiritual dignities it is said: "Amen, amen, I say to you, he that entereth not by the door into the sheepfold but climbeth up another way is a thief and a robber."[272] Therefore, they who commit simony are thieves.

B. Reasons stealing is forbidden
Thou shalt not steal. This Commandment, as has been said, forbids taking things wrongfully. We can bring forth many reasons why it is given.

1. The gravity of the sin
The first is because of the gravity of this sin, which is likened to murder: "The bread of the needy is the life of the poor; he that defraudeth them thereof is a man of blood."[273] And again: "He

---

[269] Lev. 19:35-36
[270] Ps. 14:1,5 (RSV: Ps. 15:1,5)
[271] Job 20:15
[272] John 10:1
[273] Ecclus. 34:25 (RSV: Sir. 34:21)

that sheddeth blood and he that defraudeth the laborer of his hire are brothers."[274]

2. The unique dangers of theft

Stealing is forbidden because of the peculiar danger involved in theft: no sin is so dangerous. After committing other sins a person may quickly repent. For instance, a person can repent of murder when his anger cools or of fornication when his passion subsides. But even after he repents of stealing, it is still hard to make the necessary satisfaction by fulfilling the obligation of restitution and the duty to make up for the loss incurred by the rightful owner.

These duties are above and beyond the obligation to repent of the sin itself: "Woe to him that heapeth together that which is not his own! How long doth he load himself with thick clay!"[275] For a person cannot easily extricate himself from thick clay.

3. The uselessness of stolen goods

Stealing is also forbidden because of the uselessness of stolen goods, for they are of no spiritual value: "Treasures of wickedness shall profit nothing."[276] Wealth can indeed be useful for almsgiving and offering of sacrifices, for "the ransom of a man's life are his riches."[277] But it is said of stolen goods: "I am the Lord who loves judgment and hates robbery in a holocaust."[278] And again: "He that offereth sacrifice of the goods of the poor is as one that sacrificeth the son in the presence of his father."[279]

[274] Ecclus. 34:27 (RSV: Sir. 34:22)
[275] Hab. 2:6
[276] Prov. 10:2
[277] Prov. 13:8
[278] Isa. 61:8
[279] Ecclus. 34:24 (RSV: Sir. 34:20)

4. The loss of spiritual goods

Finally, stealing is forbidden because the results of theft are peculiarly harmful to the thief, since they lead to his loss of other goods. It is not unlike the mixture of fire and straw: "Fire shall devour their tabernacles, who love to take bribes."[280] And it ought to be known that a thief may lose not only his own soul, but also the souls of his children, since they, too, are bound to make restitution.

[280]Job 15:34

VIII

THE EIGHTH COMMANDMENT
Thou shalt not bear false witness against thy neighbor.

The Lord has forbidden anyone to injure his neighbor by deed. In this Commandment he forbids us to injure him by word: *Thou shalt not bear false witness against thy neighbor.*[281]

A. Ways of bearing false witness
False witness may be given either in a court of justice or in ordinary conversation:

1. In a court of justice
In the court of justice, it may happen in three ways, according to the three persons who may violate this Commandment in court.

a. A false accusation by the plaintiff: "Thou shalt not be a detractor nor a whisperer among the people."[282] Note well that it is not only wrong to speak falsely, but also to conceal the truth: "If thy brother shall offend against thee, go and rebuke him."[283]

---

[281] Cf. Aquinas, *Summa Theologiae*, II-II, Q. 122, art. 6
[282] Lev. 19:16
[283] Matt. 18:15

65

b. A lie told by a witness: "A false witness shall not be un-punished."[284] This Commandment includes all the preceding ones, inasmuch as the false witness may himself be the murderer or the thief, and as such should be punished according to the Law.

"When after most diligent inquisition they find that the false witness hath told a lie against his brother, they shall render to him as he meant to do to his brother. . . . Thou shalt not pity him, but shalt require life for life, eye for eye, tooth for tooth, hand for hand, and foot for foot."[285] Again: "A man that beareth false witness against his neighbor is like a dart and a sword and a sharp arrow."[286]

c. An unjust sentence by the judge: "Thou shalt not . . . judge unjustly. Respect not the person of the poor, nor honor the countenance of the mighty. But judge thy neighbor according to justice."[287]

2. In ordinary conversation

In ordinary conversation, we can violate this Commandment in five ways:

a. By detraction: "Detractors . . . are hateful to God."[288] Here the phrase *hateful to God* implies that nothing is as dear to a person as his good reputation: "A good name is better than great riches."[289] Detractors take away this good name: "A serpent bites in silence, but he that backbiteth secretly is no

---

[284] Prov. 19:5
[285] Deut. 19:18-21
[286] Prov. 25:18
[287] Lev. 19:15
[288] Rom. 1:30
[289] Prov. 22:1

better."[290] Thus, if detractors do not restore a man's reputation, they cannot be saved.

b. By listening to detractors willingly: "Hedge in thy ears with thorns, hear not a wicked tongue, and place doors and bars on thy mouth."[291]

We should not listen deliberately to such things, but ought to turn away, showing a sad and stern countenance: "The north wind driveth away rain as doth a sad countenance a backbiting tongue."[292]

c. By gossiping: By repeating whatever they hear, gossipers break this precept: "Six things there are which the Lord hateth, and the seventh His soul detesteth: . . . him that soweth discord among brethren."[293]

d. By flattery: By speaking honeyed words, flatterers bear false witness: "The sinner is praised [by flatterers] in the desires of his soul, and the unjust man is blessed."[294] And again: "O my people, they that call thee blessed, the same shall deceive thee."[295]

e. By lying: The prohibition against bearing false witness applies to every form of falsehood: "Be not willing to make any manner of lie, for the custom thereof is no good."[296]

---

[290] Eccles. 10:11
[291] Ecclus. 28:28 (RSV: Sir. 28:24-25)
[292] Prov.25:23
[293] Prov. 6:16,19
[294] Ps. 10:3
[295] Isa. 3:12
[296] Ecclus. 7:14 (RSV: Sir. 7:13)

B. Reasons lying is forbidden

1. Lying likens a person to the Devil, because a liar is as the son of the Devil. Now we know that a man's speech reveals the region and country of his origin. Thus: "Even thy speech doth discover thee."[297] In the same way, some men are of the Devil's kind; and because they are liars, they are called *sons of the Devil*, since the Devil is "a liar and the father of lies."[298] Thus the Devil lied when he said, "No, you shall not die the death."[299]

In contrast, some other men are the children of God (who is Truth). These are the men who speak the truth.

2. Lying ruins society. Men live together in society, but this is soon rendered impossible if they do not speak the truth to one another. "Wherefore putting away lying, speak ye the truth, every man with his neighbor; for we are members one of another."[300]

3. Lying destroys the liar's reputation for the truth. He who is accustomed to telling lies is not believed, even when he speaks the truth: "What can be made clean by the unclean? And what truth can come from that which is false?"[301]

4. Lying kills the liar's soul, for "the mouth that belieth killeth the soul."[302] And again: "Thou wilt destroy all that speak a lie."[303]

[297] Matt. 26:73
[298] John 8:44
[299] Gen. 3:4
[300] Eph. 4:25
[301] Ecclus. 34:4 (RSV: Sir. 34:4)
[302] Wisd. of Sol. 1:11
[303] Ps. 5:7 (RSV: Ps. 5:6)

Accordingly, it is clear that lying is a mortal sin (although it must be known that some lies may be venial).

It is a mortal sin, for instance, to lie in matters of faith. This concerns professors, prelates, and preachers, and is the gravest of all other kinds of lies: "There shall be among you lying teachers who shall bring in sects of perdition."[304] Then there are those who lie to wrong their neighbor: "Lie not to one another."[305] These two kinds of lies, therefore, are mortal sins.

C. Reasons people lie

1. For personal advantage
There are some who lie for their own advantage, and this in a variety of ways.

a. Out of humility, people sometimes lie. This may be the case in confession, about which St. Augustine says: "Just as one must avoid concealing what he has committed, so also he must not mention what he has *not* committed." "Hath God any need of your lie?"[306] And again: "There is one that humbleth himself wickedly and his interior is full of deceit; and there is one that humbleth himself exceedingly with a great lowness."[307]

b. Because of shame, people sometimes lie, such as when someone tells a falsehood believing that he is telling the truth and then, on becoming aware of it, he is ashamed to retract

---

[304] 2 Pet. 2:1
[305] Col. 3:9
[306] Job 13:7
[307] Ecclus. 19:23-24 (RSV: Sir. 19:26)

the falsehood. "In no wise speak against the truth, but be ashamed of the lie of thy ignorance."[308]

c. For desired results, people sometimes lie, such as when they wish to gain or avoid something: "We have placed our hope in lies and by falsehood we are protected."[309] And again: "He that trusteth in lies feedeth the winds."[310]

2. To benefit another, people sometimes lie, such as when they wish to free someone from death, danger, or some other loss. This must be avoided, as St. Augustine tells us: "Accept no person against thy own person, nor against thy soul a lie."[311]

3. Out of vanity, people sometimes lie. This, too, must never be done, lest the habit of such lead us to mortal sin: "For the bewitching of vanity obscureth good things."[312]

[308]Ecclus. 4:30 (RSV: Sir. 4:25)
[309]Isa. 28:15
[310]Prov. 10:4 (No equivalent in RSV)
[311]Ecclus. 4:26 (RSV: Sir. 4:22)
[312]Wisd. of Sol. 4:12

IX

THE NINTH (TENTH) COMMANDMENT
Thou shalt not covet thy neighbor's goods.[313]

There is this difference between divine and human law: human law judges deeds and words but divine law also judges thoughts. This is because human laws are made by men who see things only exteriorly, but divine law is from God, who sees both external things and the very interior of men. "Thou art the God of my heart."[314] And again: "Man seeth those things that appear, but the Lord beholdeth the heart."[315]

A. Commandments that concern thoughts
Therefore, having considered those Commandments which concern words and deeds, we now treat of those Commandments which concern thoughts. For with God the intention is taken for the deed. Thus, *Thou shalt not covet* is meant to include not only the *taking* by act, but also the *intention to take*. Therefore God says: "Thou shalt not [even] covet thy neighbor's goods."

---

[313] St. Thomas places the Tenth Commandment (in the present traditional enumeration) before the Ninth. The Tenth Commandment is wider in extension than the Ninth, which is specific.
[314] Ps. 72:26 (RSV: Ps. 73:26)
[315] 1 Kings 16:7 (RSV: 1 Sam. 16:7)

B. Reasons for this Commandment

There are a number of reasons for this.

1. Man's desire has no limits, because desire itself is boundless. But he who is wise will aim at some particular end, for no one should have aimless desires: "A covetous man shall not be satisfied with money."[316] But the desires of man are never satisfied, because the heart of man is made for God.

Thus, says St. Augustine: "Thou hast made us for Thee, O Lord, and our heart is restless until it rests in Thee."[317] Therefore, nothing less than God can satisfy the human heart: "Who satisfieth thy desire with good things."[318]

2. Covetousness destroys peace of heart, which is highly delightful. The covetous man is ever solicitous to acquire what he lacks and to hold that which he has: "The fullness of the rich will not suffer him to sleep."[319] "For where thy treasure is, there is thy heart also."[320] It was for this reason, says St. Gregory, that Christ compared riches to thorns.[321]

3. Covetousness makes riches useless to the wealthy and to others, because the covetous desire only to hold on to them: "Riches are not comely for a covetous man and a niggard."[322]

4. Covetousness destroys the equality of justice: "Thou shalt not take bribes, which blind even the wise and pervert the words

---

[316] Eccles. 5:10
[317] St. Augustine, *Confessions*, 1.1
[318] Ps. 102:5 (RSV: Ps. 103:5)
[319] Eccles. 5:12
[320] Matt. 6:21
[321] Luke 8:14
[322] Ecclus. 14:3 (RSV: Sir. 14:3)

of the just."[323] And again: "He that loveth gold shall not be justified."[324]

5. Covetousness destroys the love of God and neighbor. For, as St. Augustine says, "The more one loves, the less one covets." Also, the more one covets, the less one loves. "Nor despise thy dear brother for the sake of gold."[325] And just as "No man can serve two masters," so neither can he serve "God and mammon."[326]

6. Covetousness produces all kinds of wickedness. It is "the root of all evil," says St. Paul, and when this root is implanted in the heart it brings forth murder and theft and all kinds of evil: "They that will become rich fall into temptation and into the snare of the Devil and into many unprofitable and hurtful desires which drown men in destruction and perdition. For the desire for money is the root of all evil."[327] And note, furthermore, that covetousness is a mortal sin when one covets one's neighbor's goods without reason; and even if there be a reason, it is a venial sin.

---

[323] Exod. 23:8
[324] Ecclus. 31:5 (RSV: Sir. 31:5)
[325] Ecclus. 7:20 (RSV: Sir. 7:18)
[326] Matt. 6:24
[327] 1 Tim. 6:9-10

X

THE TENTH (NINTH) COMMANDMENT
Thou shalt not covet thy neighbor's wife.

St. John says that "all that is in the world is the concupiscence of the flesh, the concupiscence of the eyes, and the pride of life."[328] Now all that is desirable is included in these three, two of which are forbidden by the precept: "Thou shalt not covet thy neighbor's house."[329] (Here *house*, signifying "stature," refers to avarice, for "glory and wealth shall be in his house."[330] This means that he who desires his neighbor's *house*, desires honors and riches.) Thus, after the precept forbidding desire for the house of one's neighbor (i.e., honor and riches) comes the Commandment prohibiting concupiscence of the flesh: *Thou shalt not covet thy neighbor's wife.*

A. Occasions when sin rules in the flesh
Because of the corruption which resulted from the Fall, none have been free from this concupiscence except Christ and the glorious Virgin. Yet, wherever there is concupiscence, there is either venial

---

[328]1 John 2:16
[329]The text of Exod. 20:17 (which contains the Ninth and Tenth Commandments) reads as follows: "Thou shalt not covet thy neighbor's house; neither shalt thou desire his wife, nor his servant, nor his handmaid, nor his ox, nor his ass, nor anything that is his."
[330]Ps. 111:3 (RSV: Ps. 112:3)

75

or mortal sin — if it is allowed to dominate the reason. Hence the precept does not say, "Let sin not be." For it is written: "I know that there dwelleth not in me (i.e., in my flesh) that which is good."[331]

1. When concupiscence reigns in the heart (by our consenting to it), sin rules in the flesh. Therefore St. Paul adds "so as to obey the lusts thereof" to the words: "Let not sin reign in your mortal body."[332] Accordingly the Lord says: "Whosoever shall look on a woman to lust after her, hath already committed adultery with her in his heart."[333] For with God, the intention is taken for the act.

2. When our heart's concupiscence is expressed in words, sin rules in the flesh: "Out of the abundance of the heart the mouth speaketh."[334] And again: "Let no evil speech proceed from your mouth."[335] Therefore, one is not without sin who composes titillating songs. Even the philosophers thought this, and poets who wrote amatory verses were sent into exile.

3. When our members are made to serve iniquity (at the behest of desires), sin rules in the flesh: "You have yielded your members to serve uncleanness and iniquity unto iniquity."[336] These, therefore, are the progressive steps of concupiscence.

B. How concupiscence can be overcome

We must realize that the avoidance of concupiscence demands much labor, for concupiscence is grounded in something within us.

---

[331] Rom. 7:18
[332] Rom. 6:12
[333] Matt. 5:28
[334] Matt. 12:34
[335] Eph. 4:29
[336] Rom. 6:19

It is as hard as trying to capture an enemy in one's own household. However, there are four ways to overcome concupiscence.

1. By fleeing its external occasions (such as, for instance, bad company and whatever else may be an occasion for this sin), concupiscence can be overcome: "Gaze not upon a maiden lest her beauty be a stumbling block to thee. . . . Look not around about thee in the ways of the city, nor wander up and down in the streets thereof. Turn away thy face from a woman dressed up and gaze not about upon another's beauty. For many have perished by the beauty of a woman, and hereby lust is enkindled as a fire."[337] And again: "Can a man hide fire in his bosom and his garments not burn?"[338] Therefore, Lot was commanded to flee: ". . . neither stay thou in all the country about."[339]

2. By mortification of the flesh and by not giving an opening to thoughts which of themselves are the occasion of lustful desires, concupiscence can be overcome: "I chastise my body and bring it into subjection."[340]

3. By perseverance in prayer, concupiscence can be overcome: "Unless the Lord build the house, they labor in vain who build it."[341] Also: "I knew that I could not otherwise be continent, except God gave it."[342] Again: "This kind is not cast out save by prayer and fasting."[343]

---

[337] Ecclus. 9:5-9 (RSV: Sir. 9:5-8)
[338] Prov. 6:27
[339] Gen. 19:17
[340] 1 Cor. 9:27
[341] Ps. 126:1 (RSV: Ps. 127:1)
[342] Wisd. of Sol. 8:21
[343] Mark 9:29

All this is not unlike a fight between two persons, one of whom you desire to win, the other to lose. You must sustain the one and withdraw all support from the other. So, also, between the spirit and the flesh there is a continual combat. Now if you wish the spirit to win, you must assist it by prayer and resist the flesh by such means as fasting (for by fasting the flesh is weakened).

4. By keeping oneself busy with wholesome occupations, concupiscence is overcome: "Idleness hath taught much evil."[344] Again: "This was the iniquity of Sodom thy sister: pride, fullness of bread, abundance, and idleness."[345] St. Jerome says: "Be always busy in doing something good, so that the Devil may find you ever occupied." Moreover, as he tells us, study of the Scriptures is the best of all occupations: "Love to study the Scriptures and you will not love the vices of the flesh."

---

[344]Ecclus. 33:29 (RSV: Sir. 33:27)
[345]Ezek. 16:49

XI

SUMMARY OF THE COMMANDMENTS

So these are the ten precepts to which our Lord referred when He said, "If thou wilt enter into life, keep the Commandments."[346] There are two main principles of these Commandments: love of God and love of neighbor.

A. Love of God
If we are to love God, we must necessarily do three things:

1. We must have no other God
In support of this is the Commandment, *Thou shalt not have strange gods before me.*

2. We must give God all honor
Thus it is commanded: *Thou shalt not take the name of the Lord thy God in vain.*

3. We must freely take our rest in God
Hence: *Remember that thou keep holy the Sabbath day.*

---

[346]Matt. 19:17

B. Love of neighbor
To love God worthily, we must first of all love our neighbor.

1. We must honor our parents
So we have the Commandment, *Honor thy father and thy mother.*

2. We must refrain from harming our neighbor

a. By act
Thus we have those Commandments which forbid harm to our neighbor in act: *Thou shalt not kill* concerns our neighbor's person; *Thou shalt not commit adultery* concerns the person united in marriage to our neighbor; and *Thou shalt not steal* concerns our neighbor's external goods.

b. By word and by thought
We are also commanded to avoid injury to our neighbor both by word (*Thou shalt not bear false witness*) and by thought (*Thou shalt not covet thy neighbor's goods* and *Thou shalt not covet thy neighbor's wife*).

THE SACRAMENTS

I

THE SACRAMENTS IN GENERAL

We shall first consider the sacraments of the Church under one heading, since they all pertain to the effects of grace.

A. The nature of a sacrament

1. A sacrament is a sign of a sacred thing

First, we must know that which St. Augustine wrote in the tenth book of *The City of God*: "a sacrament is a sacred thing" or "the sign of a sacred thing."[347] Even in the Old Law there were certain sacraments (i.e., signs of sacred things) such as the paschal lamb and other legal, sacred signs (or sacraments) which, however, did not *cause* grace but only signified or indicated the grace of Christ.

The Apostle calls these sacraments "weak and needy elements."[348] They were *needy* because they did not contain grace and *weak* because they could not confer grace. As St. Augustine says, in them the merits of Christ brought about salvation in a more hidden manner under the cover of visible things.

---

[347] St. Augustine, *City of God*, 10.5
[348] Gal. 4:9

2. A sacrament is a visible form of an invisible grace

The sacraments of the New Law, on the other hand, both contain grace and confer it. A sacrament of the New Law is a visible form of invisible grace. Thus, the exterior washing which takes place when water is poured in Baptism represents that interior cleansing which takes away sin by virtue of the sacrament of Baptism.

B. The number of the sacraments

There are seven sacraments of the New Law: Baptism, Confirmation, the Eucharist, Penance, the Anointing of the Sick, Holy Orders, and Matrimony. The first five of these sacraments are intended to bring about the perfection of the individual man in himself; the other two — Holy Orders and Matrimony — are so constituted that they perfect and multiply the entire Church.

C. The effects of the sacraments

The spiritual life conforms to the physical life. In the physical life man is perfected in three chief ways: (1) *by generation,* in that he is born into this world; (2) *by growth,* through which he is brought up into stature and perfect strength; and (3) *by food,* which sustains his life and powers. This would suffice were it not that man falls ill and then needs his health to be restored (4) *by healing.* These same needs are found in the spiritual life:

1. Regeneration

First, man needs that regeneration or rebirth which is brought through the sacrament of Baptism: "Unless a man be born again of water and the Holy Spirit, he cannot enter into the kingdom of God."[349]

---

[349]John 3:5

2. Spiritual growth

Secondly, it is necessary that man develop perfect strength which is, as it were, a spiritual growth. This, indeed, comes to him in the sacrament of Confirmation. It is like the strengthening which the Apostles received when the Holy Spirit came upon them and confirmed them. The Lord had said to them: "But stay you in the city of Jerusalem till you be endued with power from on high."[350]

3. Nourishment

The third similarity is that man must be fed with spiritual food through the sacrament of the Eucharist: "Unless you eat the flesh of the Son of Man and drink His blood, you shall not have life in you."[351]

4. Spiritual healing

Fourthly, man must be healed spiritually through the sacrament of Penance: "Heal, O Lord, my soul, for I have sinned against Thee."[352]

5. Bodily and spiritual healing

Fifth, man is healed both in soul and in body in the sacrament of the Anointing of the Sick: "Is any man sick among you? Let him bring in the priests of the church and let them pray over him, anointing him with oil in the name of the Lord. The prayer of faith shall save the sick man and the Lord shall raise him up; and if he be in sins, they shall be forgiven him."[353]

[350]Luke 24:49
[351]John 6:53
[352]Ps. 40:5 (RSV: Ps. 41:4)
[353]James 5:14-15

6. The good of the Church

Finally, two sacraments — Holy Orders and Matrimony — were instituted for the common good of the Church. Through the sacrament of Holy Orders, the Church is ruled and spiritually multiplied. Through Matrimony, it is increased physically in numbers.

D. Characteristics of all the sacraments

The seven sacraments have some things which they all hold in common and some things which are proper to each one.

1. The conferring of grace is common to each sacrament.

2. Words and physical acts are essential to each sacrament. Christ, the author of the sacraments, is the Word made flesh. Just as the flesh of Christ was sanctified and has the power of sanctifying because of the Word united to itself, so also the sacraments are made holy and have the power of sanctifying through the words which accompany the action. Thus, St. Augustine says: "The word is joined to the element and the sacrament is made."[354]

a. The form of a sacrament consists of the words by which that sacrament is sanctified.

b. The matter of a sacrament consists of those things which are sanctified. Water, for example, is the *matter* of Baptism, and holy chrism is the *matter* of Confirmation.

[354]St. Augustine, *In Joan.*, *Tract.* 80.3

3. A minister is required for each sacrament. The minister confers the sacrament with the intention of doing that which the
Church intends.

The sacrament is not brought into being if any one of these
three requirements is lacking (i.e., if there is lacking the due form
of the words, if the matter is not present, or if the minister does
not intend to confer the sacrament).

4. The interior disposition of the recipient plays a role in each
sacrament. Thus, the effect of the sacrament can be impeded
through the fault of the recipient, such as when a person feigns
to receive it but has a heart unprepared to receive it worthily.
Although he actually receives the sacrament, such a person does
not receive the effect of the sacrament: the grace of the Holy
Spirit. "For the Holy Spirit of discipline will flee from the
deceitful."[355] On the other hand, however, there are some who
never receive sacramentally, yet who receive the effect of a
sacrament because of a devotion toward the sacrament which
they may have in desire or in a vow.

E. Unique characteristics of particular sacraments
There are some things which are characteristic of each individual
sacrament.

1. Sacraments which impress a character on the soul
Certain sacraments impress on the soul a character which is a
certain spiritual sign distinct from the other sacraments. Such
are the sacraments of Holy Orders, Baptism, and Confirmation.
A sacrament which impresses character on the soul is never

---

[355]Wisd. of Sol. 1:5

repeated in a person who has once received it. Thus, he who is baptized need never again receive this sacrament. Neither can he who has been confirmed receive Confirmation again, nor he who has been ordained repeat his ordination. The reason is that the character which each of these sacraments impresses is indelible.

2. Sacraments which do not impress a character on the soul

In the other sacraments, however, a character is not impressed on the recipient. Hence they can be repeated as far as the person is concerned, but not as far as the matter is concerned. Thus, one can frequently receive Penance, frequently receive the Eucharist, and can be anointed more than once with the Anointing of the Sick. Likewise, a person can be married more than once.

Yet, regarding the matter, the same Host cannot be frequently consecrated, nor ought the oil of the sick be frequently blessed.

II

THE SACRAMENTS IN PARTICULAR

Having considered the sacraments in general, it is now necessary to say something about each one in particular.

A. Baptism

First we consider Baptism, about which the following must be known:

1. The matter of Baptism is natural water, and it makes no difference whether it is cold or warm. One cannot, however, baptize in artificial waters (such as rose water).

2. The form of Baptism is: "I baptize thee in the name of the Father and of the Son and of the Holy Spirit."

3. The minister of Baptism ordinarily is the priest, whose office it is to baptize. In case of necessity, however, not only a deacon but also any lay person (even a pagan or a heretic) can baptize as long as he observes the form specified by the Church and intends to act according to the intention of the Church.

If someone is baptized by such persons but *not* in a case of necessity, he has received the sacrament and must not again be baptized, but the grace of the sacrament was not received because such persons are not truly deputed to baptize other than in cases of necessity. Hence, they act contrary to the law of the Church regulating the sacraments.

4. The effect of Baptism is to remit both actual sin and Original Sin as well as all guilt and punishment which they incur. No kind of punishment must be enjoined for past sins upon those just newly baptized. Hence those who die immediately after Baptism are admitted to the glory of God without delay. Therefore the effect of Baptism is the opening of the gates of Paradise.

5. Errors concerning Baptism have arisen:

a. The Solentiani received a baptism not of water but of the spirit. Against them the Lord says: "Unless a man be born again of water and the Holy Spirit, he cannot enter into the kingdom of God."[356]

b. The Donatists rebaptized those baptized by Catholics. Against them is written: "One faith, one baptism."[357]

c. Those who claim that a man in the state of sin cannot baptize also err. Against them it is said: "He upon whom thou shalt see the Spirit descending and remaining upon Him, He it is that baptizeth."[358]

It is thus seen that a minister who is himself evil does not invalidate either this or any of the other sacraments because

[356] John 3:5
[357] Eph. 4:5
[358] John 1:33

it is Christ who, by the merits of His Passion, gives to each sacrament its efficacy; and He is good.

d. The Pelagians err when they say that children are not freed from Original Sin by baptism, but rather through their baptismal regeneration are merely admitted as adopted children of God into the Kingdom, being translated from a good state to a better one.

B. Confirmation

1. The matter of Confirmation is chrism made from oil (signifying the bright luster of conscience) and from balsam (signifying the odor of a good name). Both oils are blessed by the bishop.

2. The form of Confirmation is: "I sign thee with the sign of the Cross and I confirm thee with the chrism of salvation, in the name of the Father and of the Son and of the Holy Spirit. Amen."

3. The minister of Confirmation is solely the bishop. It is not licit for a priest to anoint on the forehead with chrism those who are to be confirmed.[359]

4. The effect of Confirmation is that the Holy Spirit is imparted to give strength, just as the Holy Spirit was given to the Apostles on the day of Pentecost. Thus, the Christian must boldly confess the name of Christ.

The person who is confirmed is anointed on the forehead (wherein is the seat of fear) so that he will not blush to confess

---

[359] In the Latin Church, the ordinary minister of Confirmation is the bishop. However, in virtue of Canon 882, a priest can also validly confer this sacrament in certain circumstances.

91

either the name of Christ or especially the Cross of Christ, which to the Jews was a scandal and to the pagans foolishness. For this reason, he is signed with the sign of the Cross.

5. Errors concerning Confirmation: Certain Greeks have erred about this sacrament by saying that it could be administered by one who is only a priest.

Against this it is said that the Apostles sent the Apostles Peter and John to impose hands upon those who had been baptized by Philip the deacon, and they received the Holy Spirit. Now the bishops of the Church are in the places of the Apostles; and in their place also do they impose hands when the sacrament of Confirmation is administered.

C. The Holy Eucharist

1. The matter of the Eucharist is wheaten bread and wine made from the grape mixed with a little water so that the water becomes part of the wine. The water signifies the faithful who are incorporated into Christ. The *matter* for this sacrament cannot be anything other than wheaten bread and wine from the grape.

2. The form of the Eucharist is the very words of Christ: "This is my body" and "This is the cup of my blood, the blood of the new and everlasting covenant, the mystery of faith, which shall be shed for you and for many, so that sins may be forgiven." These words spoken by the priest in the person of Christ bring into being this sacrament.

3. The minister of the Eucharist is the priest and no one else can consecrate this matter into the Body of Christ.

4. The effects of the Eucharist

a. Christ becomes physically present

In virtue of the above words, bread is changed into the Body of Christ and wine into His Blood so that Christ is entirely contained under the appearances of bread which remain without a subject and He is entirely contained under the appearances of wine. Moreover, under each part of the consecrated host and of the consecrated wine, Christ is totally present even after the separation is made.

b. The communicant is united with Christ

In the soul of one who worthily receives this sacrament, its second effect is to bring about the union of that man with Christ, as He himself says: "He that eateth my flesh and drinketh my blood abideth in me and I in him."[360] And since man is incorporated with Christ and united to His members through grace, it follows that through this sacrament grace is increased in those who receive it worthily. Therefore, in this sacrament there are three aspects: (1) the *sacramentum tantum* (that which is the sacrament alone: the species of bread and wine); (2) the *res et sacramentum* (the true Body of Christ); and (3) the *res tantum* (the unity of the Mystical Body, the Church) which this sacrament both signifies and causes.

5. Errors concerning the Eucharist

There have been many errors regarding this sacrament.

a. Berengarius said that the true Body of Christ is not present in the Eucharist but rather the Eucharist is only a sign of it.

[360]John 6:56

Against this is written: "For my flesh is meat indeed; and my blood is drink indeed."[361]

b. The Arrodinici offer in their sacrament bread and cheese because they say that men at first made offerings of the fruits of the earth and of their flocks.

Against this, however, stands the fact that the Lord, the institutor of this sacrament, gave His disciples bread and wine.

c. The Cataphrygians and the Praeputiati drew the blood of an infant from tiny punctures in its body. Mixing this with flour, they made a bread of it. They claimed that thus they consecrated the sacrament.

This is more like the sacrifices of demons than that of Christ: "And they shed innocent blood . . . which they sacrificed to the idols of Canaan."[362]

d. The Aquarians offer water only in their sacrifices. But against this are the words from the mouth of Wisdom, which is Christ: "Drink the wine which I have mingled for you."[363]

e. The Poor People of Lyons held that any just man can consecrate the Eucharist. Against this error is the fact that the Lord gave to the Apostles the power to celebrate this sacrament. Therefore, only those who receive this power in a certain succession from the Apostles can consecrate this sacrament.

---

[361] John 6:55
[362] Ps. 105:38 (RSV: Ps. 106:38)
[363] Prov. 9:5

D. Penance[364]

1. The matter of Penance consists, as it were, of the acts of the penitent, which are called the three parts of Penance.

a. Heartfelt contrition is the first part, by which the sinner is sorry for the sins he has committed and determines not to sin again.

b. Confession is the second part. In it the sinner confesses to the priest all the sins of which he is mindful and all of them at one time to one priest, not dividing them among a number of priests.

c. Satisfaction is the third part, which is enjoined according to the judgment of the priest and which consists especially in fasting, prayer, and almsgiving.

2. The form of Penance consists of the words of absolution which the priest speaks when he says: "I absolve thee."

3. The minister of Penance is the priest having authority to absolve, which authority is either ordinary or by commission of his superior.

4. The effect of Penance is absolution from sin.

5. Errors concerning Penance: The Novatians say that any one who has sinned after having been baptized cannot receive pardon through the sacrament of Penance. Against this are the words:

---

[364]Or *Confession*, now called *Reconciliation*

"Be mindful therefore from whence thou art fallen; do penance and do the first works."[365]

E. The Anointing of the Sick

1. The matter of the Anointing of the Sick is olive oil blessed by the bishop. This sacrament should only be received by those who are in danger of death through sickness. They are to be anointed in the places of the five senses: on the eyes, because they are the organs of sight; on the ears, because of hearing; on the nostrils, because of smell; on the lips, because of taste or speech; on the hands because of touch; and on the feet because of walking.

2. The form of the Anointing of the Sick is: "Through this anointing and through His most divine mercy, may the Lord forgive thee whatever thou hast committed through sight . . . " (and so on for the other senses).

3. The minister of the Anointing of the Sick is the priest.

4. The effect of the Anointing of the Sick is healing for both mind and body.

5. Errors concerning the Anointing of the Sick: It is said that the Elaeonitae anointed their dying with oil, balsam, and water and that they accompanied the anointing with invocations in Hebrew pronounced over the head of the sick. However, this is contrary to the form handed down by St. James, as given above.

[365]Rev. 2:5

F. Holy Orders

There are seven orders: priesthood, diaconate, subdiaconate, aco-
lyte, exorcist, lector, and porter. Tonsure (clerkship, *clericatus*) is not
an order, but a formal profession of giving one's life to the divine
ministry. The episcopate is rather a dignity than an order.

1. The matter of Holy Orders is that matter which is handed
over to the candidate at the conferring of the order. Thus, for
example, priesthood is conferred by the handing over of the
chalice. Likewise, each order is conferred by the handing over of
that matter which in a special way pertains to the ministry of
that particular order.

2. The form of Holy Orders is this: "Receive the power to offer
sacrifice in the Church for the living and the dead." Similarly,
power is conferred in the other orders.

3. The minister of Holy Orders is the bishop who confers the
orders.

4. The effect of Holy Orders is an increase of grace for the
performance of the duties of a worthy minister of Christ.

5. Errors concerning Holy Orders: Arius erroneously taught
that the priesthood could not be distinguished from the episcopate.

G. Matrimony

Matrimony is a sign of the union between Christ and the Church.

1. The efficient cause of Matrimony is the mutual consent expressed in words effective in the present by the parties.

2. The threefold good of Matrimony includes:

a. The birth of children and their education to the worship of God.

b. Fidelity, which one spouse must render to the other.

c. Its sacramental character. The indivisibility of Matrimony shows forth the indivisible union of Christ and His Church.

3. Errors concerning Matrimony

a. Tatian condemned marriage. Against such it is written: "If thou take a wife, thou hast not sinned."[366]

b. Jovinian erroneously made marriage equal to virginity.

c. The Nicolaitians mutually exchanged their wives. There were also many other heretics who taught and worked impurities. Against them are the words of St. Paul: "Marriage honorable in all, and the bed undefiled."[367]

---

[366] 1 Cor. 7:28
[367] Heb. 13:4

III

THE GIFTS OF THE SACRAMENTS

By the reception of these seven sacraments, man is led to future eternal glory which consists in seven gifts: three of the soul and four of the body.

A. The three gifts of the soul

1. The vision of God in His essence is the first gift given to the soul, according to the words: "We shall see Him as He is."[368]

2. Comprehension, or the understanding of God as the reward of our merits, is the second gift of the soul: "So run that you may obtain."[369]

3. Perfect enjoyment is the third gift of the soul, wherein we shall have full happiness in God: "Then shalt thou abound in delights of the Almighty, and shalt lift up thy face to God."[370]

---

[368] 1 John 3:2
[369] 1 Cor. 9:24
[370] Job 22:26

B. The four gifts of the body

1. Impassibilty[371] is the first gift which shall be enjoyed by the body, for "this corruptible must put on incorruption."[372]

2. Brilliancy is the second gift of the body: "Then shall the just shine as the sun in the kingdom of their Father."[373]

3. Agility is the third gift of the body, through which those saved can instantly be present wherever they wish: "They shall run to and fro like sparks among the reeds."[374]

4. Subtlety is the fourth gift of the body, whereby those saved can penetrate wherever they desire: "It is sown a natural body; it shall rise a spiritual body."[375]

To all of which may He lead us,
who liveth and reigneth forever and ever!
Amen.

---

[371] The state of being beyond the reach of suffering or harm
[372] 1 Cor. 15:53
[373] Matt. 13:43
[374] Wisd. of Sol. 3:7
[375] 1 Cor. 15:44

BIOGRAPHICAL NOTE

ST. THOMAS AQUINAS (1225-1274)

Scholar *and* saint! Certainly it's a rare combination in our day, but St. Thomas Aquinas was both. He devoted his entire life to comprehending God's Revelation — through reason, contemplation, and prayer — and to living in conformity with the call of that Revelation.

Born of an illustrious and politically prominent family in Naples, St. Thomas was educated at the famous Monte Cassino Abbey and at the University of Naples. In 1244, against the wishes of his family, he entered the Dominican Order.

The Dominicans sent Thomas to the University of Paris to study with the renowned Aristotelian scholar, Albert the Great. In 1252, Thomas began his teaching career which involved him in every major intellectual debate of the time. Through many formal academic disputations, through his preaching, and in over 100 written volumes, St. Thomas gave his reason unreservedly to the service of Christian Revelation. Relying heavily on the Greek philosopher Aristotle, Thomas showed that Christian faith is credible, defensible, and intelligible.

Moreover, St. Thomas's prodigious scholarship nurtured his own spiritual development. He prayed intensely and was known to suffer the terrible spiritual trials and sublime consolations of the true ascetic and contemplative.

St. Thomas died on March 7, 1274 at the age of fifty. He was canonized in 1323 and proclaimed a Doctor of the Universal Church in 1567.

In his encyclical *Æterni Patris* (August 4, 1879), Pope Leo XIII called on all men to "restore the golden wisdom of St. Thomas and to spread it far and wide for the defense and beauty of the Catholic Faith, for the good of society, and for the advantage of all sciences."

APPENDIX

The following pages constitute a *complete* outline of each of the sections of this book and include subheadings not found in the Table of Contents. Use this outline as a guide in reading and studying the text.

THE COMMANDMENTS

APPENDIX

 B. Anger
  1. Anger and killing
  2. Obligations regarding anger
   a. Be not quickly provoked to anger
    1. Anger is virtuous only sometimes
     a. The wise man is properly subject to moderate anger
      1. Christ was angry sometimes
      2. Anger sometimes has a good purpose
     b. The kinds of anger
      1. Anger can be a judgment of reason
      2. Righteous anger
      3. Sinful anger
       a. Mortally sinful anger
       b. Venially sinful anger
    2. Anger diminishes freedom
   b. Do not remain angry long
   c. Control the intensity of your anger
   d. Do not let wrath explode in angry words
   e. Do not let anger lead to evil deeds

 A. Adultery
  1. Adultery of the wife
   a. Infidelity to the Law of God
   b. Infidelity to her husband
   c. Theft
  2. Adultery of the husband
   a. Violation of the equality of rights between spouses
   b. Defect of strength
   c. Undermining the authority of the husband
 B. Fornication and impurity
 C. Married intercourse
  1. For procreation
  2. For mutual comfort
  3. For the excitement of lust
  4. For illicit ends
 D. The prohibition of adultery and fornication
  1. They destroy the soul
  2. They destroy life
  3. They waste substance
  4. They defile offspring
  5. They destroy honor

APPENDIX

THE SACRAMENTS